Modern Middle East Nations
AND THEIR STRATEGIC PLACE IN THE WORLD

LEBANON

Tripoli

Zghartā

Al Hirmil

LEBANON

Orontes River

Mediterranean Sea

Jūniyah

Ba'labakk

34°N

Beirut

Zahlah

L E B A N O N   M O U N T A I N S

SYRIA

Bekaa Valley

Saydā
(Sidon)

Marj 'Uyun

Litani River

Sūr
(Tyre)

Jordan River

33°N

ISRAEL

Sea of Galilee

E

36°E

N

W   E

S

0   10   20 Miles

0   10   20 Kilometers

Conic Projection

Modern Middle East Nations
AND THEIR STRATEGIC PLACE IN THE WORLD

LEBANON

JAN McDANIEL

MASON CREST PUBLISHERS
PHILADELPHIA

Produced by OTTN Publishing, Stockton, New Jersey

Mason Crest Publishers
370 Reed Road
Broomall, PA 19008
www.masoncrest.com

3 5 7 9 8 6 4 2

Library of Congress Cataloging-in-Publication Data

McDaniel, Jan.
  Lebanon / Jan McDaniel.
      p. cm. — (Modern Middle East nations and their strategic
place in the world)
Summary: Discusses the geography, history, economy, government,
religion, people, foreign relations, and major cities of Lebanon.
Includes bibliographical references and index.
  ISBN 1-59084-511-0
1. Lebanon—Juvenile literature. [1. Lebanon.] I. Title. II. Series.
DS80 .M39 2003
959.92—dc21
                                                   2002013003

Modern Middle East Nations
AND THEIR STRATEGIC PLACE IN THE WORLD

TABLE OF CONTENTS

Modern Middle East Nations

AND THEIR STRATEGIC PLACE IN THE WORLD

Dr. Harvey Sicherman, president and director of the Foreign Policy Research Institute, is the author of such books as *America the Vulnerable: Our Military Problems and How to Fix Them* (2002) and *Palestinian Autonomy, Self-Government and Peace* (1993).

Introduction

by Dr. Harvey Sicherman

Situated as it is between Africa, Europe, and the Far East, the Middle East has played a unique role in world history. Often described as the birthplace of religions (notably Judaism, Christianity, and Islam) and the cradle of civilizations (Egypt, Mesopotamia, Persia), this region and its peoples have given humanity some of its most precious possessions. At the same time, the Middle East has had more than its share of conflicts. The area is strewn with the ruins of fortifications and the cemeteries of combatants, not to speak of modern arsenals for war.

Today, more than ever, Americans are aware that events in the Middle East can affect our security and prosperity. The United States has a considerable military, political, and economic presence throughout much of the region. Developments there regularly find their way onto the front pages of our newspapers and the screens of our television sets.

Still, it is fair to say that most Middle Eastern countries remain a mystery, their cultures and religions barely known, their peoples and politics confusing and strange. The purpose of this book series is to change that, to educate the reader in the basic facts about the 23 states and many peoples that make up the region. (For our purpose, the Middle East also includes the North African states linked by ethnicity, language, and religion to the Arabs, as well as Somalia and Mauritania, which are African but share the Muslim religion and are members of the Arab League.) A notable feature of the series is the integration of geography, demography, and history; economics and politics; culture and religion. The careful student will learn much that he or she needs to know about ever so important lands.

A few general observations are in order as an introduction to the subject matter.

The first has to do with history and politics. The modern Middle East is full of ancient sites and peoples who trace their lineage and literature to antiquity. Many commentators also attribute the Middle East's political conflicts to grievances and rivalries from the distant past. While history is often invoked, the truth is that the modern Middle East political system dates only from the 1920s and was largely created by the British and the French, the victors of World War I. Such states as Algeria, Iraq, Israel, Jordan, Kuwait, Saudi Arabia, Syria, Turkey, and the United Arab Emirates did not exist before 1914—they became independent between 1920 and 1971. Others, such as Egypt and Iran, were dominated by outside powers until well after World War II. Before 1914, most of the region's states were either controlled by the Turkish-run Ottoman Empire or owed allegiance to the Ottoman sultan. (The sultan was also the caliph or highest religious authority in Islam, in the line of the prophet Muhammad's successors, according to the beliefs of the majority of Muslims known as the Sunni.) It was this imperial Muslim system that was ended by the largely British military victory over the Ottomans in World War I. Few of the leaders who emerged in the wake of this event were happy with the territories they were assigned or the borders, which were often drawn by Europeans. Yet, the system has endured despite many efforts to change it.

The second observation has to do with economics, demography, and natural resources. The Middle Eastern peoples live in a region of often dramatic geographical contrasts: vast parched deserts and high mountains, some with year-round snow; stone-hard volcanic rifts and lush semi-tropical valleys; extremely dry and extremely wet conditions, sometimes separated by only a few miles; large permanent rivers and *wadis*, riverbeds dry as a bone until winter rains send torrents of flood from the mountains to the sea. In ancient times, a very skilled agriculture made the Middle East the breadbasket of the Roman Empire, and its trade carried luxury fabrics, foods, and spices both East and West.

Most recently, however, the Middle East has become more known for a single commodity—oil, which is unevenly distributed and largely concentrated in the Persian Gulf and Arabian Peninsula (although large pockets are also to be found in Algeria, Libya, and other sites). There are also new, potentially lucrative offshore gas fields in the Eastern Mediterranean.

This uneven distribution of wealth has been compounded by demographics. Birth rates are very high, but the countries with the most oil are often lightly populated. Over the last decade, Middle East populations under the age of 20 have grown enormously. How will these young people be educated? Where will they work? The failure of most governments in the region to give their people skills and jobs (with notable exceptions such as Israel) has also contributed to large out-migrations. Many have gone to Europe; many others work in other Middle Eastern countries, supporting their families from afar.

Another unsettling situation is the heavy pressure both people and industry have put on vital resources. Chronic water shortages plague the region. Air quality, public sanitation, and health services in the big cities are also seriously overburdened. There are solutions to these problems, but they require a cooperative approach that is sorely lacking.

A third important observation is the role of religion in the Middle East. Americans, who take separation of church and state for granted, should know that most countries in the region either proclaim their countries to be Muslim or allow a very large role for that religion in public life. Among those with predominantly Muslim populations, Turkey alone describes itself as secular and prohibits avowedly religious parties in the political system. Lebanon was a Christian-dominated state, and Israel continues to be a Jewish state. While both strongly emphasize secular politics, religion plays an enormous role in culture, daily life, and legislation. It is also important to recall that Islamic law (*Sharia*) permits people to practice Judaism and Christianity in Muslim states but only as *Dhimmi*, protected but very second-class citizens.

Fourth, the American student of the modern Middle East will be impressed by the varieties of one-man, centralized rule, very unlike the workings of Western democracies. There are monarchies, some with traditional methods of consultation for tribal elders and even ordinary citizens, in Saudi Arabia and many Gulf States; kings with limited but still important parliaments (such as in Jordan and

Morocco); and military and civilian dictatorships, some (such as Syria) even operating on the hereditary principle (Hafez al Assad's son Bashar succeeded him). Turkey is a practicing democracy, although a special role is given to the military that limits what any government can do. Israel operates the freest democracy, albeit constricted by emergency regulations (such as military censorship) due to the Arab-Israeli conflict.

In conclusion, the MODERN MIDDLE EAST NATIONS series will engage imagination and interest simply because it covers an area of such great importance to the United States. Americans may be relative latecomers to the affairs of this region, but our involvement there will endure. We at the Foreign Policy Research Institute hope that these books will kindle a lifelong interest in the fascinating and significant Middle East.

Tanks and military vehicles line a street in Beirut, Lebanon, in August 1982. Between 1975 and 1990, Lebanon was devastated by civil war, invasion by Israel, and occupation by Syrian forces.

Place in the World

ebanon, the gateway to the Middle East, is a country rich in both natural beauty and cultural heritage. A small nation at the junction of three continents—Europe, Africa, and Asia—Lebanon has historically been a bridge between the cultures of the East and West. Since ancient times, this region has been important for trade and military strategy. A parade of conquering civilizations has left the imprint of different cultures.

In many ways, Lebanon is distinctive in the Arab world. Its population has a larger percentage of Christians, and its culture reflects more Western influences, than any other country in the Arab world. In fact, Lebanon was once known as the "Switzerland of the Middle East." It boasts a highly literate population that is friendly, industrious, and politically sophisticated. Many Lebanese speak several languages, including English. Unlike other Arab nations in the **arid**

Middle East, Lebanon has an abundance of water; however, it lacks significant resources of oil. With its mountains, Lebanon is the only Middle Eastern country offering winter skiing and snowboarding.

But since the 1970s Lebanon has been devastated by political conflicts and 15 years of civil war, resulting in Syrian political control of the country. An entire generation has grown up amidst upheaval. The war brought constant danger, instability, terrorism, the destruction of homes and property, and the deaths of many people. Many Lebanese remain numb or angry from the violence and uncertainty of a war in which neighbor often fought neighbor.

Before the civil war began in 1975, Lebanon was prosperous and modern, on friendly terms with the United States and other Western nations as well as with fellow Arab countries. Foreign investors were drawn to Beirut's banks and tourists visited its beaches. Outsiders mistakenly viewed Lebanon as a place where Christians and Muslims lived together in harmony. But deep-seated conflicts between religious sects, political factions, and the rich and the poor were already brewing.

Today Lebanon faces the challenge of rebuilding and reclaiming independence. The war reduced Beirut to ruins. Renovation and reconstruction began in the 1990s. Tourist attractions have reopened and cultural events resumed. Efforts are also underway to clean up an environment spoiled by pollution. As a result, Lebanon looks toward restoring the hope of a better life for future generations. Yet mistrust and internal conflict linger. Religious minorities worry about their survival. Because loyalty first to family, religion, and village is deeply ingrained in Lebanese society, national unity is difficult to achieve. Reconciliation programs bring former enemies together, getting both sides talking in an attempt to heal old wounds.

As westerners became the target of terrorist attacks during the civil war, Lebanon came to be regarded as a dangerous place.

The United States did not allow its citizens to visit the country and closed its embassy. For Lebanon to encourage foreign investment, the development of new businesses, and a renewal of tourism, the country must overcome its bad reputation. The war also plunged Lebanon into an economic crisis. Today, the country struggles with a high cost of living, unemployment, and an astronomical national debt. With jobs scarce, nearly one-third of Lebanese citizens—many bright and talented professionals—are seeking visas to immigrate to other countries.

Since the creation of Israel in 1948, Lebanon has been near the center of violence in the Middle East. Lebanon borders Israel, and when the Jewish state was established thousands of displaced Arab Palestinians poured into Lebanon. Unable to go home, some became **militant** during the 1960s, resorting to terrorism. Over the years Palestinian forces have used the country as a base to launch attacks against the Israelis—resulting in retaliatory attacks by Israeli forces. Guerrilla activity has also heightened internal conflicts, caused property damage, and distracted attention from domestic problems. Today, more than 380,000 Palestinian refugees occupy "temporary" camps in Lebanon. Some Lebanese sympathize deeply with their plight, while others want them to leave.

The anti-Israel organization **Hezbollah** operates freely within Lebanon. The Lebanese government considers it a resistance organization, while the United States deems it a terrorist group. Syria, listed by the United States as a country that supports terrorism, sent in troops to end Lebanon's civil war. Lebanon remains dominated by Syria; thousands of Syrian soldiers are still occupying the country. Other countries have asked Lebanon and Syria to control Palestinian and Hezbollah attacks on Israel while the diplomats pursue peace.

The Lebanese, whatever their troubles, see their own fate bound up in the resolution of larger regional conflicts. They continue to believe that they can play a useful role in helping the diplomacy. After hosting a March 2002 Arab League Summit in Beirut, Lebanon was one of five countries selected to present a Middle East peace initiative to Israel. Saudi Arabian Crown Prince Abdullah proposed an exchange of normal relations with Arab countries for return of Arab lands seized in 1967 and creation of an Arab Palestinian state. U.S. President George W. Bush has challenged moderate Arab leaders to become more involved in the peace process. Optimists hope pressure from both sides will force a truce between the Palestinians and Israelis.

As the volatile Middle East continues to dominate world events, Americans may feel puzzled by what is happening and why. Just as Arabs harbor misconceptions about the United States, the American public frequently misunderstands the ways of the Middle East. Mistaken assumptions about the Arab world and the West stem from lack of understanding the cultural differences. Approaches to negotiation, justice, and settling differences are different in Arab culture. Understanding the current situation in Lebanon reveals much about ongoing conflicts in the Middle East.

Terrorist acts in the name of religion are not new to the Middle East, but Westerners became targets only during the later years of the 20th century. The events of September 11, 2001, changed many Americans' view of the world. The Lebanese government condemned the terrorist attacks on the World Trade Center and the Pentagon, and helped the United States by arresting suspected al-Qaeda terrorists. Outside the U.S. Embassy in Beirut, Lebanese students lit candles to mourn the victims. Most Arab countries have worked with American intelligence agencies to find and arrest Islamic extremists.

For many Arabs, September 11 changed perceptions as well. Terrorists represent one extremist faction in Arab culture. Islamic militant extremist groups have hurt both the East and the West.

Despite its troubles, the government of Lebanon believes it has an important role to play in bringing peace to the Middle East. In March 2002, Lebanon's president, Emile Lahoud (seated, center), and foreign minister, M. Mahmoud Hamoud (right) hosted an Arab League summit in Beirut. (Seated to the left at the table is Amr Moussa, secretary-general of the Arab League.) At the meeting Saudi Arabia's crown prince proposed that the Arab League offer Israel normal relations in exchange for the recognition of a Palestinian state.

Westerners have lost confidence in the security and safety of Middle Eastern countries, while Arabs in general feel unwelcome in the West. In May 2002, Lebanese Prime Minister Rafik Hariri told an audience at the Arab Investment and Capital Markets Conference in Beirut, "The West's perception of Arabs is now one of suspicion and distrust. The truth is that an Arab visitor to the West is now surrounded by a question mark."

The writings of the famous Lebanese-American poet Kahlil Gibran, which have been translated into many languages, expressed a vision of understanding and harmony between America and the Arab world. With understanding, perhaps someday that harmony will come.

The view from this hillside at Qasr Naous, in northern Lebanon, is spectacular. Visitors can see Lebanon's famous cedar trees, as well as Roman ruins, in the ancient city.

The Land

Smaller overall than the state of Connecticut, Lebanon features a dramatic landscape of snowcapped mountains and sandy beaches touching the Mediterranean Sea. The name "Lebanon" comes from the Semitic word *laban*, which means white, signifying the snowfall in the mountains. Traveling to any location within the tiny country requires a drive of only a few hours.

Part of what is known as the **Levant**, the territory at the eastern end of the Mediterranean that also includes Israel and Syria, Lebanon links land and sea routes between Europe, Asia, and Africa. Ports at Beirut, Sidon (in Arabic Sayda), and Tyre (Sur) have made the country historically important for commercial trade.

About 120 to 135 miles (193 to 217 kilometers) north to south and 50 miles (81 km) east to west at its widest point, Lebanon comprises some 4,015 square miles (10,395 square kilometers). It borders Syria in the east and north and Israel in the south. At present, there is no official border with Israel. The **Blue Line** mapped out by United Nations cartographers separates Lebanon and Israel. The formal boundary will be determined when a peace agreement is reached.

FOUR GEOGRAPHIC REGIONS

Geographically, Lebanon consists of four parts. A narrow plain runs about 140 miles (225 km) along the coast, interrupted at some points by mountains reaching to the sea. The country's interior consists of two parallel mountain ranges running north and south with a valley between them.

The narrow plain along the coast with its rocky beaches and bays is the location of the main cities and farms. At its widest point, along the border with Syria, the coastal plain stretches a mere eight miles (13 km). Summers here are hot and extremely humid. The high humidity makes it feel hotter. The average rainfall is about 35 inches (89 centimeters) per year, and heavy dews help water crops. West winds blow during the day, and then wind blows out to sea at night. Temperatures average 55° Fahrenheit (13° Celsius) in January and 84°F (29°C) in June. Beirut enjoys a Mediterranean climate similar to the climate of southern California, with about 300 days of sunshine per year. While snow is plentiful in the mountains, it is rare as far south as Beirut. To escape the summer heat, many families living in Beirut move to summer homes in the mountains where the cool dry air and lower humidity make daytime feel cooler and temperatures are lower at night. Winters are short and mild. Spring and autumn are also short seasons. Temperatures are lower farther inland and there is less humidity.

The Lebanon Mountains (the region historically known as **Mount Lebanon**) run parallel to the coast and extend about 100 miles (161 km). Fruit has been grown on stone terraces built along steep

A map showing Lebanon's major geographic features. A narrow coastal plain moves inland from the Mediterranean. It gradually rises to the country's major mountain range, the Lebanon Mountains. On the other side of these mountains is the fertile Bekaa Valley, which is bordered to the west by a second mountain range, the Anti-Lebanon Mountains.

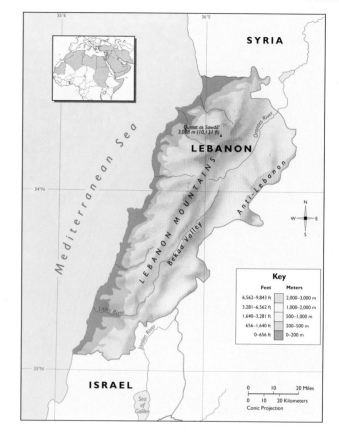

mountainside slopes since the 19th century. At the higher elevations, mountain springs irrigate crops. The soil is Middle Eastern *terra rosa*, red earth. The mountains can receive as much as 50 or 60 inches (127 to 152 cm) of annual precipitation. Heavy snow sometimes remains into summer. Lebanon's rugged mountains have provided refuge to persecuted religious groups. Establishing settlements in the high elevations, they remained free to follow their customs without interference, as their tormentors were unlikely to pursue them through the rough terrain.

Lebanon's highest peak, Qurnat as Sawda', or Black Horn, is in the Lebanon Mountains southwest of Tripoli near the village of Bsharri. Visitors can reach the top via a ski lift, a rough track for four-wheel drive vehicles, or a climbing path. From the top, at 10,131 feet (3,088 meters), there is a panoramic view of the coast.

Jounieh is one of many beautiful Lebanese cities on the Mediterranean coast. Visitors can water ski in the bay, or travel a half-hour to snow ski in the nearby mountains.

On a clear day, visitors with sharp eyes might be able to see the island of Cyprus off the coast of Turkey.

The Bekaa Valley between the two mountain ranges and along the eastern border is about 5 to 10 miles (8 to 16 km) wide. Summers here are hot and dry with cooler nights. Winter is cold, wet, and windy. This central plateau constitutes the country's main agricultural region. Just over 30 percent of Lebanon is agricultural land. Farmers grow sugar beets, potatoes, grapes, and herbs and medicinal plants. In addition, illegal drug crops, particularly hashish, are sometimes cultivated here. The area receives less rain than the mountains do, but has a plentiful water supply for crop irrigation from rivers and mountain springs.

The plateau transforms into low rolling hills in the south near the foothills of Mount Hermon. At 9,230 feet (2,815 m), this volcano is the highest peak of the Anti-Lebanon Mountains. This range runs along the eastern border and extends into Syria and Israel.

The Litani River flows south, then travels west through a gorge and into the Mediterranean. The 90-mile-long (145 km) river is used for irrigation and hydroelectric power generation. The hydro-electric project in the Bekaa Valley section of the Litani River is Lebanon's largest power facility. The Orontes River (or Nahr al-Asi, "Rebel River") flows north across Syria then into Turkey. Springs along the porous western slopes of the Lebanon Mountains supply plentiful water.

An aerial view of farms in Lebanon's Bekaa Valley region. This valley between the country's two mountain ranges is Lebanon's main agricultural area.

Part of the country lies over an earth fault prone to quakes, sometimes of devastating intensity. For example, a series of earthquakes in the sixth century destroyed Roman temples at Baalbek, damaged Tyre and Sidon, and killed approximately 30,000 residents of Beirut.

Easterners and Westerners alike have marveled over the natural splendor of Lebanon's Jeita Caverns, a vast cave complex that consists of two levels with an underground river flowing through the bottom. About 15 miles (24 km) north of Beirut, the complex is more than three miles (5 km) long. An American missionary named William Thompson discovered the lower level in 1836. Thompson happened upon the cave, but ventured only a short way inside; instead, he fired a gun and judged by the echoes that the cave com-

The Geography of Lebanon

Location: Middle East, bordering the Mediterranean Sea between Israel and Syria
Total Area: smaller than the state of Connecticut
    total: 4,015 square miles (10,395 square kilometers)
    land: 3,950 square miles (10,227 square kilometers)
    water: 65 square miles (168 square kilometers)
Borders: Israel 49 miles (79 kilometers); Syria 233 miles (375 kilometers); coastline, 140 miles (225 kilometers)
Climate: mild to cool, wet winters with hot, dry summers; heavy winter snows in the mountains
Terrain: narrow coastal plain; Bekaa Valley separates Lebanon and Anti-Lebanon Mountains
Elevation extremes:
    lowest point: Mediterranean Sea 0 feet (0 meters)
    highest point: Qurnat as Sawda' 10,131 feet (3,088 meters)
Natural hazards: dust storms, sandstorms

Source: Adapted from CIA World Factbook, 2002.

plex was huge. Later, American, French, and English explorers probed deeper inside. Many wrote their names on "Maxwell's Column," a limestone pillar near the entrance.

The Lebanese began exploring the caverns in the 1940s and discovered the upper galleries in 1958. The upper grotto features pinkish limestone deposits, crystals, abundant stalactites and stalagmites, flowing stone draperies, canyons, and sinkholes. After a gangplank was constructed, the upper level opened to tourists in 1969. Concerts and other cultural events have been held inside the caves.

The lower level's subterranean river is the principal source for the Nahr el-Kalb, or Dog River. A waterfall flows at the entrance. Illuminated by electric lights, the lower level opened to the public in 1958. Tourists ride by boat through green water with a constant temperature of 60°F (15°C). The lower level sometimes closes in winter due to high water. The caves closed in the mid-1970s due to the Lebanese civil war; after some renovation work, they were reopened in July 1995.

THE FAMOUS CEDAR AND OTHER RESOURCES

Today Lebanon possesses few mineral resources except limestone, which is quarried extensively. The country's once-rich copper mines were exhausted long ago.

About 4 percent of Lebanon is forest today. Gone are most of the legendary cedars that once covered the upper slopes of the Lebanon Mountains along with cypress, pine, and oak trees. Through the centuries, intensive logging has depleted the forests.

The cedar remains the national symbol; it is pictured on Lebanon's flag to represent enduring strength. The cedars of Lebanon are mentioned in the Bible and other ancient writings. Lebanon cedars have distinctive broad branches that spread up to 50 feet (15 meters), and the trees can grow as tall as 100 feet (31 meters).

Snow-covered cedars in the Lebanon Mountains. The tree has become a national symbol.

Various invaders have prized the cedar wood since ancient times when the first settlers, the Phoenicians, used it to build merchant ships. Other conquerors used cedar wood to build temples and tombs. The Roman Emperor Hadrian attempted to protect the cedar forests by placing carved stone boundary markers around them. Two of some 200 markers found in modern times are displayed in the American University of Beirut Museum. In the Middle Ages, villagers cleared trees from farmland and either used the wood for building or burned it as firewood. During World War I, 60 percent of the trees in Lebanon were cut, mostly by Turks to build railroads and to fuel steam engines. During World War II, British and French troops used cedar wood to build a railroad from Tripoli to Haifa.

Today, the mountain slopes grow mainly brush, pine, and cypress. In recent years, the government has taken steps to protect remaining cedar stands from both man and beast (goats enjoy grazing on cedar saplings). To increase the number of trees, additional cedars have been planted, but they grow very slowly. Only after 40 years does a cedar produce new seeds.

In Barouk's famous cedar forest, a protective wall encloses 350-year-old cedars. Lebanon's oldest cedar grove, Arz el Rab, or Cedars of the Lord, grows in the center of a mountain village, Bsharri. Some of the trees are believed to be as much as 1,500 years old. In 1843, a **Maronite** chapel was built in center of the forest. In 1876, Great Britain's Queen Victoria financed construction of a protective stone wall around them. Hundreds of new trees have been planted over the past 30 years. Deadwood has been removed, the soil fertilized, and lightning rods installed to protect the trees from damage caused by electrical storms.

In 2002, the Coca-Cola Company planted 150 cedar trees in the former Israeli-occupied South Lebanon village of Jezzine. The fledgling forest, called CedaRoots, tops the village's highest hill—which had to first be cleared of more than 500 land mines. Another 350 saplings will be planted by September 2004. The neighboring village of Rihan planted 2,000 cedars the previous year.

A July 1996 law established Al-Shouf Cedar Reserve, which occupies 5 percent of the entire country in the Shouf Mountains south of Beirut and in the western Bekaa Valley. The law aims to protect existing cedars and increase the number of trees. The reserve skirts nine rural villages. No hunting is allowed, and the area is home to 27 species of wild mammals, 104 species of birds, and 124 species of plants. Some of these species, such as wolves, hyenas, foxes, and lynx, are considered rare. Two other protected areas have been established. Horsh Ehden Reserve in the northern Lebanon Mountains includes cedars, junipers, maples, and wild apple trees. It provides sanctuary for native and migratory birds, mammals, and various reptiles and amphibians such as lizards, turtles, frogs, toads, and newts. Palm Island Reserve off the coast of Tripoli constitutes an eastern Mediterranean marine nature habitat. It encompasses the islands of Palm, Sanani, and Remakin and the surrounding sea.

During the civil war, dynamiting drove away Lebanon's sea turtle population. The number of sea turtles, which benefit the environment by stabilizing algae and jellyfish (sea turtles are the only natural predator of jellyfish), is declining. Often turtles are accidentally snared in fishing nets. Construction along Lebanon's coast has left little sand for the turtles to lay eggs. When turtles do find open space, crabs, stray dogs, or human gourmets frequently dig up the eggs. Lebanon's Agriculture Ministry has banned the killing of sea turtles; however, this ruling has not yet become a law. Lebanon's government has been reluctant to impose costly measures on fishermen, such as limiting the fishing season or requiring the use of "turtle-friendly" but more expensive silk nets, because of the country's economic problems.

A DAMAGED ENVIRONMENT

The degradation of Lebanon's environment has become a concern. Before the civil war, the country had no restrictions on dumping sewage and industrial waste into the ocean. As a result Lebanon's northern beaches—especially those near power stations—suffer from water pollution. Cleaner public beaches lie farther south, at Mansouri, Tyre, and Jbeil. The Mansouri beach boasts some of Lebanon's cleanest water. The beach at Tyre belongs to a government-protected area but awaits city action to clean up litter strewn across the beach.

Air pollution has also become a problem, particularly around Beirut, because of exhaust from vehicles as well as fumes from fuel oil burned to operate power plants.

Toward the end of 20th century, the government committed

Members of an explosive ordinance disposal unit carefully make their way through a minefield near Fatma Gate in southern Lebanon. During years of occupation and war, an estimated 400,000 mines were planted in the region. They must be cleared before Lebanese farmers can return to their homes.

itself to environmental conservation and cleanup. Recently, the United Nations joined with private corporations to launch a "Go Green" program, which promotes corporate social responsibility toward the environment. In 1998, the government announced a plan to replace fuel oil with natural gas at the electric plants. Low-quality fuel used in cars spews smoky exhaust, so in 2001 Lebanon's Car Owners Association called for cleaner fuel and strict standards on exhaust emissions.

Since June 2000, Israel has provided the United Nations with maps showing locations of some 400,000 land mines around its former military outposts and along the Blue Line. The United Nations has pressed for additional maps showing mines between the Litani River and Jezzine. A 6-year-old South Lebanese boy was killed in April 2002 when he mistook a cluster bomblet he found for a ball. Operation Emirates Solidarity, funded by $50 million donated by the United Arab Emirates, has taken charge of clearing the area of unexploded mines, bombs, and shells.

Tourists walk through the impressive remains of the Roman temple at Baalbek, which were built at the intersection of several major trade routes in the Bekaa Valley. The history of civilization in Lebanon stretches back more than 5,000 years.

History

*T*he origin of Lebanon's first known settlers remains something of a mystery. They arrived around 3000 B.C. and established independent city-states along the Eastern Mediterranean coast in modern-day Lebanon, Syria, and Israel. Well-known as seafaring merchants, they excelled at craftsmanship and trade. In Tyre, they processed shellfish to extract a purple dye called *phoinikies*; cloth dyed with this color became prized by royalty throughout the ancient world. The Greeks called these people Phoenicians (from the Greek word for blood-red, *phoinos*).

Since the founding of the Phoenician city-states, many civilizations have conquered and influenced Lebanon. For a time, Lebanon was ruled by Egypt. In the 12th century B.C., Lebanon became independent and remained free until the Assyrians, invaders from present-day Iraq, arrived and conquered the region. The Assyrians were brutal rulers; they remained in power from 867 to 612 B.C. When the Assyrian Empire fell, Lebanon came under Babylonian rule until the Persian Empire (based in what today is the country of Iran), defeated the Babylonians around 538 B.C. By 332 B.C., Alexander the Great, the young king of Macedonia, had conquered the Persian Empire and its provinces in the Mediterranean basin. His rule brought Greek influence to Lebanon's language, literature, and philosophy. After Alexander died in 323 B.C., his generals fought over the division of his empire. Seleucus I, one of Alexander's generals, became the ruler of the Lebanon region; he and his descendants ruled until 64 B.C., when the Roman general Pompey conquered Syria and Lebanon, bringing them into the Roman Empire. Under Roman rule, Lebanon prospered and stabilized politically. The Romans

Bronze figurines covered in gold leaf from the Temple of the Obelisks in Byblos, an ancient Phoenician city. The Phoenicians established Lebanon's earliest civilization more than 5,000 years ago.

When the Romans arrived in Lebanon in 64 B.C., they built large temples, baths, and other public buildings. Many Roman ruins, such as this theater built near the sea, can still be seen.

built palaces, temples, bridges, harbors, canals, and paved roads. They also established a law school in Beirut.

When a new religion emerged in the Roman lands of the Middle East, the Romans at first attempted to suppress its practice. Christianity may have been introduced in Lebanon as early as A.D. 35 (Jesus may in fact have preached in southern Lebanon). The first Christians were persecuted for refusing to worship the Roman emperor as a god. Despite this, the new religion gradually became accepted throughout the empire. In A.D. 313 the Roman emperor Constantine the Great legalized Christianity. In 392 Christianity became the empire's official religion.

Three years later, the Roman Empire was divided after Emperor Theodosius died, leaving one son to rule the West and one to rule the East. Lebanon became part of the Eastern Roman (or Byzantine) Empire, which was ruled from Constantinople, in present-day

Turkey. Rome fell to invading Germanic tribes during the fifth century, but the Byzantine Empire remained strong in the East.

NEW RELIGIONS, NEW CONFLICTS

The Middle East would be forever altered by the emergence of another new religion—Islam, which was established during the seventh century by an Arab named Muhammad, who said he was a prophet from God. He lived on the Arabian Peninsula to the southeast of the Lebanon region. The teachings of Muhammad were compiled in a book called the Qur'an (sometimes spelled Koran),

The remains of the great Umayyad palace at Aanjar, with the Anti-Lebanon mountains in the background. The Umayyads were the first great Arab dynasty of Muslim caliphs, wielding great power throughout the Arab world from A.D. 661 to 750.

and those who followed this new religion were called Muslims. Around 634, the Muslims declared a **jihad**, or holy war, against non-Muslims living in the Mediterranean basin. They wanted to gain new territories and to spread their religion. As the Muslims moved into the region, some Arabs, tired of high Byzantine taxes and harsh treatment, welcomed them and embraced Islam. Islam spread along the Mediterranean coast. Aramaic, a language used in the Middle East since ancient times, was soon replaced by Arabic, the language of the Qur'an.

Members of many ethnic and religious groups retreated to Lebanon. At first, the Muslims did not persecute those who refused to convert. In exchange for paying a special tax, Christians were allowed to keep their faith. However, within 100 years the Muslims had toughened their attitudes toward Christians and others they considered **infidels**. They attacked non-Muslims and confiscated churches and other property. Many Christians found refuge in the rugged Lebanon Mountains. In 750, Muslim soldiers burned mountain villages and destroyed Christian churches in Lebanon. Fighting between Christians and Muslims would continue, on and off, for the next six centuries.

In 1095, Christian Pope Urban II proclaimed the first **Crusade** to recapture the Holy Land and save sites sacred to Christians, such as the Holy Sepulcher, a church in Jerusalem believed to be the site of Jesus' tomb. Western European Christians, many of them French and German knights, fought to reclaim the region from the Muslims. When the Crusaders conquered Lebanon in 1099, they were surprised to find Arab Christians there. Most Lebanese were not receptive to the European knights, believing the crusaders had come to take Arab lands. However, Lebanon's Maronites welcomed the French and other Christians, establishing links that affect Lebanon's language and culture today.

By 1300, the Muslims had reclaimed the Holy Land. The

The remains of the Crusader sea castle in Sidon, the largest city in southern Lebanon. Sidon fell to the Crusaders in 1111, and remained under their control almost continuously until 1291. This sea castle, and others along the coast, was destroyed by the Mamluks to prevent the Crusaders from regaining a foothold in the Holy Land.

Mamluk rulers of Egypt drove the Crusaders from Lebanon in 1291. The powerful Mamluks, who adhered closely to the Muslim faith, wielded great control over the Middle East for more than 200 years. By the early 16th century, though, another major power had emerged in the region—the Ottoman Turks. In 1516, the Ottomans conquered Lebanon, and soon brought the rest of the Middle East into their empire.

FOUR HUNDRED YEARS OF OTTOMAN RULE

The Ottoman Turks ruled their enormous empire from their capital city Istanbul (formerly Constantinople). However, they allowed limited self-rule to the Arabs of the Middle East; as long as each community paid taxes to the Ottomans, local leaders remained in power. During the next four centuries Lebanon was ruled by two powerful **Druze** families, the Maans and the Shihabs.

Fakhr ad Din II, a member of the Maan family, became Lebanon's ruler in 1593. He favored Lebanese independence from the Ottoman Empire. Fakhr ad Din tried to unify the different religious groups in Lebanon by promoting religious tolerance. He also enlarged the army. Lebanon prospered, selling cotton and silk to Europe. In secret, Fakhr ad Din allied with Ferdinand I, the ruler of Tuscany (in modern-day Italy) against the Ottomans. When the Ottomans found out, they attacked Lebanon; Fakhr ad Din escaped to exile in Tuscany in 1613. He returned in 1618 and again fortified the military. To modernize Lebanon, he brought in Italian architects, engineers, and agricultural experts. He extended Lebanon's territory, built forts in Syria, and took over the Holy Land. As a stronger Lebanon edged toward independence, the Ottomans attacked again. Fakhr ad Din's army was defeated; the ruler was executed in 1635 and Ottoman rule was restored.

In 1697 the Shihabs became the ruling family of Lebanon. The most important of the Shihabs was Bashir II (1788–1840). Like his predecessor Fakhr ad Din, Bashir eventually decided to break away from the Ottoman Empire. In the 1830s, he allied Lebanon with Egypt; together, the two countries conquered the major cities of Acre and Damascus in 1832 and declared independence. Bashir was an unpopular ruler, however, and by 1840 he was removed from power by a combination of internal strife between the different religious groups and an invasion by Ottoman and British troops. Bashir went into exile and a new ruler was appointed by the Ottoman sultan.

Ottoman control was restored, but friction grew between religious sects. When war broke out between the Druze and Christians, the European powers proposed dividing Lebanon into

Christian and Druze sections. This did not stop the violence. Angry over Christians moving into the Shouf Mountains, in 1860 the Druze massacred 10,000 Maronites, Greek Catholics, and Greek Orthodox Christians. A number of European powers (France, Great Britain, Austria, and Prussia), along with Russia, landed troops in Beirut, but arrived too late to stop the bloodshed. Although the international attention forced the Ottomans to crack down on the worst abuses, corrupt rulers brought hardship and suffering. Unable to earn a living, many Christians left Lebanon.

Through the second half of the 19th century, Lebanon (and particularly Beirut) blossomed as an intellectual center. Lebanon became the best-educated country in the Arab world. Foreign missionaries founded schools. The American University of Beirut was established in 1866, followed by the French Jesuit school St. Joseph's University in 1875. A revival of Arabic literature and a publishing boom contributed to the intellectual atmosphere. In secret, Christians and Muslims formed political organizations, and Lebanese desire for independence grew.

INDEPENDENCE AND UNREST

The Ottoman Empire had been in decline since the 1500s; by the end of the 19th century the empire had lost both power and territory. A 1908 uprising by a group of young military officers (who became known in the west as the "Young Turks") and conflicts in the Balkan Peninsula (the Mediterranean region that included Greece, Bulgaria, Serbia, and Montenegro) in 1912–13 further weakened the empire.

During the First World War (1914–1918), the Ottoman Turks were one of the Central Powers, allied with Germany and Austria-Hungary against the forces of Great Britain, France, Italy, Russia, and others. During the war the Turkish army occupied Lebanon. Their blockade of Eastern Mediterranean ports caused famine,

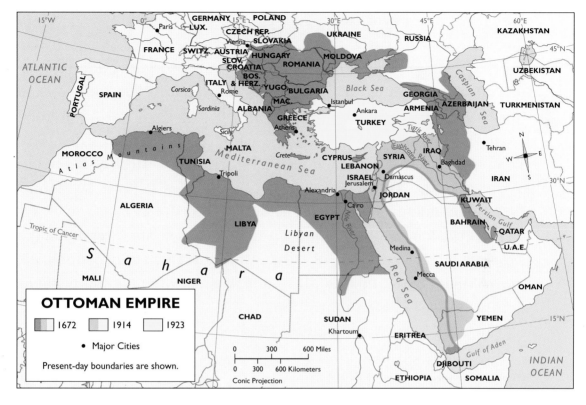

OTTOMAN EMPIRE

1672	1914	1923

• Major Cities

Present-day boundaries are shown.

0   300   600 Miles

0   300   600 Kilometers

Conic Projection

From Turkey, the powerful Ottoman Empire spread throughout the Middle East during the 16th century. By 1672 the empire controlled Lebanon and much of the rest of the Middle East, as well as large parts of north Africa, central Asia, and eastern Europe. By the start of World War I (1914) however, the empire was concentrated in the Middle East. After the war, the Ottoman territories were divided among the victorious allied powers. France received a League of Nations mandate to rule Lebanon.

especially in the mountains, and plague. Thousands of Lebanese died. The Turks disrupted mail service, cut down cedar trees to fuel military trains, and executed Syrians and Lebanese for supposed anti-Turkish activities.

After the Central Powers were defeated, the Treaty of Versailles (1919) dissolved the Ottoman Empire. Turkey would remain an independent state, but the empire's provinces would become independent—at least theoretically. The League of Nations, a world organization formed after the First World War and intended to prevent future wars through diplomacy, established these provinces as ***mandates***. The League of Nations gave certain members (particularly Great Britain and France) authority to oversee the government of these regions. In theory, the administrators of the mandates were supposed to prepare them for eventual independence and self-government; in reality, the mandated territories simply became their colonial possessions. The 1920 Treaty of San Remo temporarily gave France control of Lebanon, Syria, and the Turkish province of Antakya; a 1923 League of Nations mandate established formal French rule in Lebanon.

As a predominantly Roman Catholic country, the French rulers separated Lebanon, with its large Maronite Christian population, from Muslim Syria. In 1926, Lebanon was declared an independent republic under French protection.

During World War II, after France surrendered to the Nazi armies of Adolf Hitler in 1940, Germany controlled a reorganized French government called the Vichy government (after the city in which it was established). The Vichy regime was never recognized as a legitimate government of France by the allied forces fighting Nazi Germany; instead, the allies recognized the Free French government led by Charles de Gaulle, which opposed German occupation of France and the Vichy government. Through the Vichy government, Germany controlled France's colonies and possessions, including Lebanon. In July 1941, British and Australian forces liberated Lebanon and Syria from Vichy control. After a three-day battle at Damour (July 6–9, 1941), the Vichy government surrendered Lebanon in an armistice signed at Acre on July 13.

The people of Lebanon then asked the Free French government to end the French mandate. With pressure from other countries—including the United States, Great Britain, the Soviet Union, and other Arab nations—de Gaulle's government officially recognized Lebanese independence in 1943 (Lebanon's Independence Day is celebrated November 22). Bishara al-Khuri, a Maronite Christian, became the first president of Lebanon.

Lebanon based its government on an unwritten agreement called the National Pact or National Covenant. It called for an independent Lebanon that would be on friendly terms with the western nations as well as other Arab nations. Lebanese Christians would not depend on France, or Lebanese Muslims on Syria, for support in resolving internal problems. In an attempt to balance issues between Christians and Muslims, public offices and government jobs would be distributed according to religious quotas. Proportions were based on Lebanon's only census, which had been taken in 1932; this gave Christians political dominance and the nation's presidency.

This system might have worked if it had not been abused, but not every president ruled wisely. For example, opposition to President Khuri's strict sectarian politics sparked the formation of a reformist movement, the Social National Front. At a mass rally at Dayr al Qamar on May 17, 1952, about 50,000 protesters demanded the president's resignation. The September 11, 1952, Rosewater Revolution, a nonviolent general strike, halted activity in major cities. Khuri resigned on September 18. Amid churning hostilities, Camille Chamoun became president on September 23.

Believing Christians held an unfair share of government offices and jobs, Muslims asked for a new census. The Christians refused. Leaders of the religious groups competed for power. Christians believed ties with the West would ensure Lebanon's independence and maintain their hold on power, while Muslim Lebanese wanted stronger connections with Arab countries. In 1957, Chamoun wanted to be reelected to a second term; however, this would involve amending the national constitution. When parliamentary elections in May and June of 1957 produced enough supporters favoring the changes to the constitution, Chamoun's opponents argued that the election had been rigged.

In January 1957,
U.S. president Dwight D.
Eisenhower said the United
States would send military
assistance to nations in the
Middle East, if they asked
for it, to protect them from
Communist aggression. This
became known as the
Eisenhower Doctrine. It was
under this policy that the
marines were sent to
Lebanon in 1958.

Opposing Chamoun's pro-West policies, some Lebanese Muslims rebelled in 1958. They were encouraged by supporters of Egypt's president, Gamal Abdel Nasser, who had successfully defied the British, French, and Israelis during a standoff over the Suez Canal (1956–57). Lebanese Muslims rioted in Tripoli and Beirut. At Chamoun's request, U.S. Marines arrived in the country in July 1958, but they did not fight. The short civil war resolved nothing, although between 2,000 and 4,000 Lebanese were killed.

When General Fuad Shihab, commander of the Lebanese army, was elected president on September 27, 1958, he asked the United States to withdraw its troops.

Shihab's election brought stability to Lebanon. He maintained a neutral foreign policy of friendship both with Arab countries and the West. His administration improved roads and provided electricity, running water, and health facilities to remote villages. Charles Hilu followed him as president on August 18, 1964.

THE ROOTS OF VIOLENCE

The 1948 creation of Israel and the June 1967 Six-Day War between Israel and its Arab neighbors had brought thousands of Palestinian refugees into Lebanon. After the war, Palestinian guerrillas began attacking Israel from camps inside Lebanon. The Palestinian problem deepened hostilities between Christians and Muslims in Lebanon. While most Muslims supported the

Palestinians, Christians worried about Lebanon's security and opposed the **Palestine Liberation Organization (PLO)** and its terrorist activities. Israeli shelling along the border, in retaliation for PLO attacks, made South Lebanon a dangerous place to live. The Lebanese Army confronted the PLO guerrillas in 1969, attacking several of their bases in Lebanon. This led some Lebanese to protest in support of the Palestinians. In November, a secret agreement was negotiated in Cairo, Egypt, between the government of Lebanon and the PLO; this helped to limit guerrilla activities within the country and eased the crisis. However, guerrilla attacks—and Israeli reprisals—did not stop.

By 1972, Lebanon suffered from high inflation, unemployment, increased guerrilla activity, and public demonstrations. Martial law was declared in some areas. The government negotiated with guerrillas, prosecuted protesters, and introduced new social and economic programs. Despite this, the cycle of border attacks and retaliation continued.

On April 10, 1973, Israeli commandos raided Beirut, killing three Palestinian leaders in retaliation for the Munich Olympic

Olympic tourists and locals in Munich, Germany, protest the actions of Palestinian terrorists who held 11 members of the Israeli Olympic team hostage in September 1972. All 11 were killed. The Israeli government responded by sending commandos to Lebanon to kill Palestinian leaders—a decision that in turn angered Lebanese Muslims.

Muslim guerrilla fighters on a tank in Beirut, December 1975.

massacre, in which 11 Israeli athletes were killed by terrorist members of a Palestinian group called Black September. When the Lebanese Army did not react to this Israeli attack inside Lebanon, prime minister Saib Salam, the highest-ranking Muslim in the government, resigned. By May 1973, the Lebanese Army and the Palestinian guerrillas were engaging in battles throughout the country. Despite a declaration of martial law and a new agreement limiting guerrilla activity, the unrest continued as the Palestinians received reinforcements and aid from Syria.

TORN BY CIVIL WAR

On Sunday morning, April 13, 1975, shots were fired from a car into a church where Bashir Gemayel, leader of the Lebanese Christian militia and the **Phalangist** Party, was attending Mass.

Four people were killed. Believing the assassins were Palestinian commandos, Phalangists retaliated by ambushing a busload of Palestinians passing through a Christian neighborhood in a Beirut suburb. The 20-minute barrage of gunfire killed 27 passengers and wounded 19. Fighting erupted throughout Beirut. The Lebanese civil war had begun.

Fighting soon spread to other areas of country, where local militias, Christian and Muslim, took turns attacking each other. Concerned soldiers of both faiths defected from Lebanon's army to fight with regional factions; government leaders couldn't agree whether or not to call in the military to stop the conflict.

In Beirut residents huddled in their homes and weathered periodic shortages of water, electricity, food, and fuel. When the government tried to ration water and electricity, customers refused to pay their bills or hooked up illegally to utility lines. Those displaced by fighting in southern Lebanon moved into Beirut's abandoned, bombed-out apartments and hotels. Civilians were frequently killed, and looting and arson were common.

By November 1976, the fighting had resulted in an estimated 60,000 casualties. A rough cease-fire was imposed by the arrival of a Syrian army, bringing with it Syrian domination.

The Lebanese conflict ran deeper than just Christian versus Muslim. The battle set family against family, region against region, religion against religion, and culture against culture. With so many factions at war, identifying the enemy became difficult. Members of the Lebanese Front—mainly right-ring, anti-Palestinian Christians led by the Phalange—opposed change so they would not lose power or wealth. Those on the side of the Lebanese National Movement— mainly Muslims and poorer Christians—wanted change, a fairer distribution of power and wealth, and Arab nationalism.

Israel's invasion of Lebanon in June 1982 was intended to destroy the threat of Palestinian forces led by Yasir Arafat and his

PLO, but broadened to include supporting a new government in Beirut that would be less under Syrian control. A multinational force including U.S. Marines landed to facilitate the departure of the PLO leadership and was then withdrawn. By September 1982, Israeli troops hunting for PLO leaders had occupied Beirut. On September 14, the Phalangist leader Bashir Gemayel, an Israeli ally who had been elected president of Lebanon just three weeks earlier, was assassinated. In response, 1,000 Lebanese Christian militiamen entered the Sabra and Chatilla refugee camps in western Beirut, where they massacred more than 750 Palestinian civilians. After an investigation, Israel acknowledged that its troops had allowed the Christians into the refugee camps, but denied sanctioning the massacres, and Israeli defense minister Ariel Sharon was forced to resign.

Following the massacres the multinational force, again led by U.S. Marines, returned to Beirut, but America's second military intervention in Lebanon was no more successful than Israel's had been. The U.S. and French embassies were blown up by car bombs; in late 1983 U.S., French, and Italian military forces in Lebanon were also bombed, with heavy losses. This led to a withdrawal of foreign peacekeeping forces in Lebanon.

In February 1984, the Lebanese Army collapsed. Druze and **Shiites** soon controlled part of Beirut, and fighting persisted between the various factions, both military and political. Soon the government itself would be divided. In 1987, Lebanon's Muslim prime minister, Rashin Karami, was killed when a bomb exploded aboard a military helicopter. In September 1988, the national assembly failed to elect a successor to President Amin Gemayel (who had been elected in 1982 after his brother Bashir's death), so Gemayel appointed a Christian general, Michel Aoun, as leader of a new interim government. The Muslim leaders would not recognize Aoun's legitimacy, so Lebanon now had two governments—a

This view of the Sabra Palestinian refugee camp in west Beirut was taken in January 2001. It is estimated that more than 380,000 Palestinian refugees—most from what today is northern Israel—are living in Lebanon. They do not have the rights of citizens or access to public education. Sabra, made up of concrete buildings that lack proper electricity and modern plumbing, was the site of a brutal massacre in 1982.

Christian government headed by Aoun and a Muslim government led by Selim Hoss, Karami's successor as prime minister.

It has been said there were 1,200 ceasefires during the Lebanese civil war, and none of them lasted. Finally, the 1989 Taif Agreement, a peace plan for Lebanon that involved the major Arab states, called for constitutional changes reducing Christian power in government and the withdrawal of all foreign forces from Lebanon. The violence did not stop immediately. On November 5, 1989, Lebanon's assembly elected Rene Mouawad president; he was assassinated on November 22. Finally, the assembly elected Elias Hrawi, a Lebanese Christian, president, and approved an

The remains of the U.S. Marines barracks, destroyed by a terrorist bomb that killed 241 Marines. U.S. troops had been deployed in Beirut as part of a multinational peace-keeping force in the summer of 1982; their mission was to try to stabilize the war-torn region. After the deadly explosion in October 1983, and similar attacks on the barracks for French and Italian troops, the peacekeeping mission ended in failure the next year.

agreement to give Muslims more power.

Continued fighting caused heavy damage in Beirut as the battle lines became even more blurred. In early 1990 Aoun's supporters battled the new government and the Lebanese military, which was supported by more than 30,000 soldiers of the Syrian army. Syria, which early in the civil war had supplied weapons to the Muslim Lebanese National Movement, displeased many Lebanese Muslims by supporting the new Lebanese government, headed by a Christian. However, Syria did not want a radical nation, or one that would prompt an Israeli invasion, on its border. After heavy resistance and many casualties, the combined Syrian-Lebanese force defeated Aoun's supporters and negotiated a cease-fire. Relative calm followed but local conflicts continued in West Beirut, South Lebanon, and other areas. Periodic fighting continued between and among Christian and Muslim groups; members of Christian militias also fought Syrian troops.

With South Lebanon isolated during the war, soldiers and armed civilians had organized the South Lebanese Defense Force to defend villages against radical groups. Communications to Beirut had been cut, leaving civilians in this region on their own. In 1977, the South Lebanese Christians had allied with the Israelis for protection; they later formed the Free Lebanon Army, which opposed Hezbollah and Syrian nationalists. Members of the Free Lebanon Army received military training from the Israelis. After the Israelis withdrew their forces from southern Lebanon in 2000, more than 7,000 Arab Christians in South Lebanon, left unprotected, fled to Israel.

The Taif Agreement has been only partially successful, as a large number of Syrian troops remain in the country (the withdrawal of the Israelis in the spring of 2000 led some Lebanese, both Christian and Muslim, to demand that Syrian troops leave as well). Several armed militias, including Hezbollah in the south, observe an uneasy armistice. Since 1998, when former army commander Emile Lahoud was elected president, the Lebanese government has tried to rebuild a devastated country. During the civil war more than 100,000 people were killed, many of those children. Of the 300,000 wounded, about 100,000 remain handicapped by their injuries. Some 900,000 Lebanese were displaced from their homes, and one in five people fled the country during the war.

A Muslim mosque can be found next to a Christian church in the reborn downtown area of Beirut. During the civil war this area was part of the Green Line that divided Beirut into Christian and Muslim sections; both houses of worship have been built since the war.

Religion, Politics, and the Economy

A large Christian population represents the biggest difference between Lebanon and other Arab countries. Because so many Lebanese are Christian, Lebanon has built strong ties with the West and reflects the greatest Western influence of any Arab country. In Lebanon, religious identity often determines an individual's politics, social contacts, and education. Every Lebanese citizen carries a government-issued identity card that specifies his or her religion.

In general, it can be said that Lebanese are loyal first to their family, then to religion, then to their village, and only last to their country. Religious differences explain much about the county's political conflicts, although the politics of Lebanon are far more complex than just a division between Islam and Christianity. Within religious groups, conflicts may simmer between powerful ruling families.

Lebanon legally recognizes 17 religious branches: Alawite, Armenian Catholic, Armenian Orthodox, Chaldean, Druze, Greek Catholic, Greek Orthodox, Ismaili, Maronite, Nestorian, Protestant, Roman Catholic, Shiite Muslim, **Sunni** Muslim, Syrian Catholic, Syrian Orthodox, and Judaism (there are practically no Jews in Lebanon, however).

CHRISTIANITY IN LEBANON

From the second century A.D. until the seventh century, Christianity constituted Lebanon's major religion. Jesus is believed to have preached in Lebanon, and the apostle Paul built churches in Tyre and Sidon. Although the Romans persecuted early converts to Christianity, it eventually became the empire's official religion.

Maronites are the largest segment of Christians in Lebanon. The Maronites are followers of St. John Maron, a priest in the Uniate Church of Syria during the fourth century A.D. who broke away to found his own order. After his death, his followers fled to Lebanon's mountains and built a monastery. In 517, rival Syrian Orthodox Christians attacked the monastery and massacred 350 Maronite monks. The survivors moved farther into the mountains.

Maronites generally consider themselves Phoenicians, rather than Arabs, and favor independence. Their bond with France and the rest of the West dates to the time of the Crusades. When French Jesuits settled in Lebanon in the 16th century, they founded schools and brought French culture and customs. King Louis XIV of France appointed himself protector of Maronites in Lebanon.

In 1840, a war broke out in Mount Lebanon between the Druze and Maronites. The Druze resented the Maronites moving into the mountains and fought mercilessly. When 10,000 Christian residents of Dayr al Qamar surrendered in 1860, the Druze massacred them. Afterward, the European powers forced the Ottoman rulers to appoint a Christian governor over the Maronites.

The monastery of St. Maron, in the hills of Hermel, Bekaa Valley, was a refuge for Christians. The three-level monastery was carved from rock in the fourth century.

The Melkites, a small Christian minority, are descendants of Greek colonists who came to Lebanon to escape Arab rule between A.D. 750 and 1258. They live in northern and central Lebanon, mainly in the central Bekaa Valley. Originally the Melkites were an offshoot of the Greek Orthodox branch of Christianity, although through the influence of Roman Catholic missionaries, some eventually became Greek Catholics. Melkites consider themselves Arabs.

Armenians represent the smallest minority. In A.D. 301, Armenia (located in southwest Asia, east of Turkey) became the first Christian nation. Armenian people lived in various countries of the Middle East, but there were not many in Lebanon until the early 20th century. A slaughter of Armenians in Turkey, and upheaval during the formation of the Soviet Union (which included Armenia), led thousands to emigrate to Lebanon.

Lebanese Christian children carry torches during a special Christmas procession in the hills east of Beirut. The Christian population of Lebanon is estimated at about 1.5 million people, or approximately 40 percent of the country's total population.

The Armenians were able to integrate into Lebanese society while keeping their religious identity. Many lived in Beirut, where the Armenian section, Bourj Hamoud, was characterized by prosperous jewelers. Although other Lebanese Christians (particularly the Maronites) urged them to fight on their side when the civil war began in 1975, the Armenians tried to remain neutral. During the course of the war, Lebanese Christians battled Armenian militias for access to Bourj Hamoud. Fighting in east Beirut in early 1990 caused heavy damage to the Armenian community. Many Armenians fled to west Beirut or to the mountains, or emigrated to other countries. During the 15 years of civil war, Lebanon's Armenian population dropped by more than 50 percent; today, Armenians make up about 4 percent of the population.

One Lebanese Christian saint is St. Charbel, born Joseph Makhlouf in 1828 at Beqa-Kafra. After becoming a priest in 1859, St. Charbel lived 23 years in complete solitude and reflection. Pope Paul VI canonized him in 1977.

In May 1997 another Christian Pope, John Paul II, traveled to Lebanon—his first visit to a Middle Eastern country. Crowds of both Muslims and Christians greeted him by tossing rice or rose petals and waving Lebanese flags as he rode in a special car through the streets of Beirut. The pope celebrated an open-air mass and urged restoration of Lebanese self-rule.

Today, most Lebanese Christians oppose Arab nationalism, with its strong Islamic influences. Some favor separate Muslim and Christian sectors within Lebanon.

ISLAM IN LEBANON

The word "Islam" comes from the Arabic verb *aslama*, which means roughly to gain peace by submitting to the will of God. Islam is based on the teachings of Muhammad, born in Mecca in A.D. 570. When Muhammad was 40 years old, he began receiving revelations concerning the oneness of God (called by the Muslims Allah) and the folly of worshipping idols. These revelations are written in the Qur'an, the sacred text of Islam. Muhammad's religious teachings incorporate Arab culture. The Qur'an teaches how to conduct daily life in areas including diet and divorce laws.

Islam is based on five basic precepts, or pillars: *shahadah*, a profession of faith that there is no God but Allah, and Muhammad is the messenger of God; *salat*, a prayer performed five times a day, always facing the holy city of Mecca; *zakat*, a charitable donation to those less fortunate; *Sawm*, fasting from dawn to dusk during the month of Ramadan (the ninth month of the *hijri*, or Islamic calendar); and *hajj*, the pilgrimage to Mecca that Muslims are encouraged to make during their lifetimes.

After Muhammad's death, a split developed among his followers over who would succeed him as the Muslim leader. His only heir was his daughter, Fatimah; according to Islamic law she was not eligible to succeed him because she was a woman. Most followers supported the decision of an assembly of Muhammad's advisors, which selected a man named Abu Bakr as the first **caliph** (God's

Shiite men perform a religious ceremony in Nabatieh. To celebrate Ashura, which marks the death of Imam Hussein (the grandson of the prophet Muhammad, who is revered by Shiites) in a battle in A.D. 680, the men have slashed their heads with knives, swords, and razors to induce bleeding. Although worldwide those who follow Shi'a Islam are a minority, in Lebanon Shiites are the largest sect and make up approximately one-third of the country's population.

representative on earth). Although Abu Bakr was a close friend of Muhammad (and the father of the prophet's second wife), he was not related by blood. This indicated that the Islamic leader would be selected by the strength of his faith, not because he was descended from Muhammad. The descendants of who agreed with this decision are called Sunni Muslims.

A smaller group disagreed. They felt that Fatimah's husband Ali, who was also Muhammad's cousin, was the only rightful successor. The other group believed the caliph should be chosen from

Muhammad's descendants. Ali was eventually elected as the fourth caliph in 656; he was murdered in 661. When Ali's son did not become caliph, Ali's followers, calling themselves Shiites, broke away from the rest of the faith.

Today there are more than 1 billion Muslims worldwide. Of that number, Sunni Muslims make up more than 80 percent, while Shiites account for just about 15 percent. However, Lebanon is one of a few countries where Shiites are a larger proportion of the population. There are about 1.2 million Lebanese Shiites and 750,000 Sunni Muslims. However, a majority of the more than 380,000 Palestinian refugees living in Lebanon are Sunni Muslims.

Despite their majority status, until the second half of the 20th century most Shiites were poor farmers in southern Lebanon. They lived in small villages with substandard schools, no public transportation, and antiquated sewage disposal in trenches along the roadside. The Shiites felt ignored by Lebanon's government; many rural residents could not obtain national identity cards and lost their right to vote. The Shiites began to protest government unresponsiveness. During the 1960s and early 1970s, as fighting with Israel made life in southern Lebanon more dangerous, many Shiites moved to Beirut. Many of those who were uneducated could not find work and wound up living in slums around the city. By 1975, 250,000 Shiites were crowded within a one-quarter square mile area.

Most Shiites today favor increased political power and a unified government.

THE DRUZE IN LEBANON

The Druze live in the Shouf Mountains. Although their religion evolved from Islam in the eighth century, they are not Muslims. They broke away after Shiite Muslims in Egypt disagreed over which of the sons of Jafar al Sadik, the sixth imam, would succeed him. (In Shi'a Islam, imams are spiritual leaders.) The imam's eldest son, Ismail, was the chosen heir, but he had been caught drinking wine—a violation of Islamic law. Ismail's supporters did not believe this mistake justified his replacement by his younger brother, Musa. They broke away and became known as Ismailis. In the 11th century, some Ismailis traveled to the Lebanon Mountains where they settled and became the Druze.

Although Muslims consider the Druze infidels, or nonbelievers, the Druze believe they have preserved the core of Islam in their beliefs. However, they do not follow the teachings of the Qur'an or the five pillars of Islam. They believe in reincarnation, and have incorporated certain **Gnostic** beliefs into their theology. They regard seven as a sacred number. However, the sect is so secretive that only about 10 percent of the Druze community ever fully learn about and participate actively in the faith.

The Druze make up a small minority of Lebanon's population— about 8 percent of the total. (There are some 300,000 Druze in Lebanon; this is almost half of the worldwide Druze total.) The Druze have been persecuted periodically by members of other religions and are interested in their survival. They favor an independent Lebanon and in that respect once allied with Lebanese Christians; they distrust Sunnis, Shiites, and the West.

LEBANON'S POLITICAL SYSTEM

Lebanon was the first Arab republic to be established. It has a parliamentary system of government. Like the U.S. system, it separates executive, legislative, and judicial branches.

The legislative branch is the 128-member national assembly (called the Chamber of Deputies), which makes the nation's laws. The assembly is responsible for levying taxes and approving the budget; it also elects the president by a simple majority, and controls the Council of Ministers—the president's top advisors—by

Lebanon's 128-member Chamber of Deputies meets in this building in Beirut. The assembly is divided along religious lines, with Christians and Muslims having equal representation. Maronite Christians hold the largest number of seats (34); Shiites and Sunnis each receive 27 seats; the Druze elect 8 representatives; and minority religious groups account for the remaining seats in the assembly.

questioning members on policy issues. National Assembly members are elected by the people to serve four-year terms. The most recent parliamentary elections were held in 2002.

The president, elected by the assembly to a six-year term, appoints the prime minister; together they head the executive branch. The president can negotiate and ratify treaties and issue regulations to ensure laws are carried out. Members of the Council of Ministers—the cabinet—are appointed. The Council of Ministers oversees the operations of government.

Lebanon's judicial system is based on the Napoleonic Code, the foundation of French civil law. The system uses three levels: Courts of First Instance, Courts of Appeal, and a Court of Cassation (the equivalent of the U.S. Supreme Court). Jury trials are not used. Religious courts rule over local personal matters such as divorce and inheritance.

Lebanon is divided into six provinces, each ruled by a governor. The provinces are Beirut, North Lebanon, South Lebanon, Mount Lebanon, Nabatieh, and Bekaa. Most provinces are divided into districts, each with a district head.

THE CONFESSIONAL SYSTEM

Unlike the U.S. government system, which separates church and state, Lebanon's system bases the distribution of political power on religion. This is known as a ***confessional system***. The confessional system dates from the 1940s, as Lebanon was preparing for independence from France. Lebanese leaders agreed to an informal, unwritten National Pact, which established the system as an attempt to balance political power between Christians and Muslims by providing proportional representation for religious communities. The system was based on Lebanon's only official census, taken in 1932. Results showed a total population of 793,226, with 396,764 Christians—54,000 more Christians than Druze and Muslims. Recent population changes within Lebanon were not considered, but the census did include Lebanese citizens living outside the country—many of them Maronite Christians.

As a result the Christians held a commanding position in Lebanese politics. Under the National Pact, the president was a Maronite Christian, the prime minister a Sunni Muslim, and the speaker of the assembly a Shiite Muslim. Seats in parliament were divided between Christians and Muslims/Druze on a 6-to-5 ratio. Government hiring was also based on religion.

For decades, efforts to reform or abolish this confessional system dominated Lebanese politics. One element leading to the civil war was the struggle for political power: Muslims felt the system did not give them the representation they deserved. (Although there has been no official census, according to estimates between 50 and 70 percent of Lebanon's current population is Muslim.) At the same time, Christians wanted to hold on to their control of the assembly.

The national reconciliation accords, agreed to in October 1989 at a meeting called by the Arab League in Taif, Saudi Arabia, implemented compromises that ended the civil war. The Taif agreement called for an equal distribution of assembly seats among Christians and Muslims. Distribution of political power by religion has guaranteed representation of minority religions. Armenians, the smallest minority, are guaranteed continuous representation with several seats reserved for them.

Lebanon's flag, adopted in December 1943, features a cedar tree.

Because of the civil war, no elections were held from 1972 to 1992; instead, legislators were appointed to those seats. Angry over losing power through the Taif Accords, many Christians refused to vote in the 1992 and 1996 parliamentary elections.

POLITICAL PARTIES IN LEBANON

Political parties play a secondary role in election of candidates. The backing of a religious group, a controlling family, or a local interest group is essential to obtain a political office. The largest political parties are religious-based, some formed before Lebanon became independent. Christian political parties are most prone to internal strife.

Arabism—the belief that all Arabs share a cultural identity and should unite politically—began as a 19th-century reformist movement and became popular in the 1930s. From 1952 to 1970 the charismatic Egyptian leader Gamal Abdel Nasser promoted Arab unity in terms of culture and language. Arabism rejects the West as imperialist. In the 1960s, leftist parties formed in Lebanon to promote Arabism. Many members were Sunni Muslims. Pan-Arab parties such as Ba'ath (an Arab nationalist party that is particularly influential in Iraq and Syria), and communist and socialist groups remained active in Lebanon through the civil war.

Christian political parties include the Phalange, National Bloc,

National Liberal Party, Free Patriotic Movement, and the outlawed Lebanese Forces. The most influential Christian party, Phalange, began as a Christian youth organization. From 1937 to 1958 its membership grew from 8,000 to 50,000, and it became Lebanon's largest political organization. Attracting mainly the lower classes, the party militantly opposed Muslims and advocated Lebanese nationalism. Even before the civil war the Phalange armed and trained a militia to defend Christians from the Muslims.

The leading Druze Party is the Progressive Socialist Party. Sunni parties focus on broad issues beyond Lebanon and include Independent Nasserite Movement, the Tawhid, and Ahbash.

Shiite parties include Amal and Hezbollah. Amal was formed in 1975 to combat supposed Israeli plans to replace the Lebanese population with Palestinians. Hezbollah (or "Party of God") was organized in 1982 to drive the Israelis out of Lebanon. It considers

A volunteer counts charitable donations at the Islamic Charity Emdad Committee, one of Hezbollah's associations in Lebanon. The charity has 25,000 collection boxes throughout Lebanon, which bring in $1 million a year to be given to orphans and the poor. (Charitable giving is an important aspect of Islam, particularly Shi'a Islam.) Hezbollah, Lebanon's largest political party, runs a network of social programs for Muslims in Lebanon, which has gained the party the gratitude and support of the country's impoverished Shiite population. However, Hezbollah has also been linked to terrorist attacks against Israelis and Americans since its formation, and the party seeks to create an Islamist state.

all of Palestine occupied land and rejects Israel's right to exist. American intelligence agencies view Hezbollah as a terrorist group responsible for bombings of the U.S. Embassy and Marine barracks in Beirut, western hostage taking, and the 1985 hijacking of TWA Flight 847. Headquartered in suburban Beirut, Hezbollah has become Lebanon's largest political party. It holds nine seats in the Lebanese parliament and operates television and radio stations, schools, and hospitals.

ANGER AND FRUSTRATION

Tensions remain in Lebanon. Many Arab Christians are angry about losing power and worried about their future survival in an Arab region that is predominantly Muslim. Some believe the Syrians, now in control, favor the Muslims. Over the past ten years, sectarian ties have tightened. Members of the various religious sects seldom interact outside their own group.

Efforts are underway to bring all sides together in Lebanon. For example, the government is sponsoring a reconciliation project in the Shouf Mountains to help neighboring Druze and Christians overcome their mistrust and fear. Members of both sides sit down together to thrash out emotions over their memories of bloodshed and violence in hopes they will acknowledge each other's tragedies. The project is conducted by the Institute of World Affairs in Washington, D.C., and funded by the U.S. State Department's Office of International Religious Freedom.

The relative calm in Lebanon after implementation of the Taif Agreement in 1990 dissolved in the first half of 2002 with a string of political killings. In January of that year Elie Hobeika, a Christian warlord believed responsible for the 1982 massacre of Palestinian civilians in refugee camps, was assassinated by a car bomb. Four months later, on May 20, 2002, a Palestinian leader's son was killed in Beirut when his booby-trapped car exploded while he was driving. Lebanese police investigating the blast found the decomposing corpse of Ramzi Airani, a leader of an anti-Syrian militia, stuffed in his car trunk.

The civil war has left the Lebanese grappling with the concept of having a central government.

A STRUGGLING ECONOMY

Before the civil war, Lebanon enjoyed the highest standard of living of any Arab country. However, nearly one-third of the wealth belonged to a handful of individuals in Beirut. This 4 percent of the population consisted mainly of Maronite Christians. Many areas outside Beirut were not prosperous, although most people had at least adequate food and shelter.

Today Lebanon faces an economic crisis, and the wide gap between rich and poor remains. Some individuals found ways to capitalize on the wartime conditions, but most lost their savings as the currency (the Lebanese pound) devalued. Before the civil war started in 1975, the exchange rate was 2.3 Lebanese pounds per U.S. dollar. In 1987, the exchange rate had dropped to 250 Lebanese pounds per U.S. dollar. By 2003 the rate was holding steady at more than 1,500 Lebanese pounds to each U.S dollar. With high unemployment, inflation, and reduced buying power for the average person, Lebanon currently faces a $27 billion debt. This is more than one-and-a-half times the amount of its annual ***gross domestic product (GDP)***, the total value of all goods and services produced within a country during the year.

Historically, the industrious Lebanese have often prospered. Thousands of years ago, the Phoenicians were among the first people to base their economy on trade. In addition to being skilled artisans, the Phoenicians were the greatest seafarers of the ancient world. They sailed throughout the Mediterranean region—and perhaps as far as Africa and the East Indies—to trade their goods.

In the course of facilitating business deals, they developed a standard, simplified alphabet upon which ours is based; they also came up with the concept of double-entry bookkeeping, which is still used today.

Under the rule of the Greeks, the Phoenicians traded pistachio nuts, wine, olive oil, iron, copper, and papyrus. Lebanon prospered under Roman rule as well, producing pottery, glass, and dye and

> The Phoenicians' invention of glassblowing around 50 B.C. enabled workers to mass-produce glass objects. The process transformed glass from a luxury item to an inexpensive product common throughout households in the Roman Empire.

selling cedar, perfume, jewelry, wine, and fruit to Rome. During the Middle Ages the Lebanese exported textiles, ceramics, and glass to other Arab countries. When Lebanon was part of the Ottoman Empire, it exported silk and cotton to other parts of the empire as well as to Europe and the West.

After the French assumed the League of Nations mandate for Lebanon, the country's economy thrived, and the Lebanese enjoyed a high standard of living. The French improved the harbor at Beirut, built roads, and implemented new farming methods. They also enhanced the educational and health systems. These changes helped Lebanese entrepreneurs build successful businesses.

Interest in the Middle East and its oil resources increased after World War II. Lebanon has no significant oil resources of its own, but it became important to western nations as a major point along the oil route between the Persian Gulf and Europe. Oil pipelines were built from Saudi Arabia to Sidon in southern Lebanon and from Iraq to Tripoli on the northern coast, shortening the distance oil had to be transported. As a result, many American and European professionals were drawn to Beirut. By the 1960s, oil

Lebanese craftsmen at work. (Left) a blacksmith grinds a tool next to samples of his work. (Below) Modern power tools are used to make a lute.

production was Lebanon's only significant industry (at the time industry contributed even less to Lebanon's GDP than it does today). During that decade, Lebanon refined 14.5 million tons of imported fuel annually. However, during the civil war the pipelines ceased operation; today, the lines are still not used, and the damaged refineries are still being rebuilt.

Lebanon's Golden Era, the economic boom that began in the 1950s, mushroomed through the 1960s and 1970s. Prosperity came mainly through banking and brokerage services. Low taxes, few government regulations, and guaranteed secrecy in banking attracted Arab and Western investors. Beirut became an important financial center, home to about 100 banks. Foreign capital poured into Beirut.

The civil war devastated the economy. Unemployment rose from 5 percent in 1970 to 35 percent in the 1980s (the current rate is estimated at about 18 percent). Tourists stopped visiting the country, cutting off a vital source of income for many people. A large number of businesses closed, though some did survive (particularly banks, although banking in Lebanon also declined). Beirut's stock exchange closed in 1983 and did not reopen until 1996. The black market flourished. In maintaining services, the government accumulated a huge debt and is struggling now to pay it.

The war caused at least $25 billion in property damage. At the war's end, electricity and telephone service were out in some areas of Beirut; in certain cases service remained out into the early 1990s. Rebuilding bridges, tunnels, and roads, and restoring telephone, water, and electrical services cost around $5.5 billion.

Since the war Lebanon has undertaken a massive effort to rebuild the country, clean up the environment, and enforce laws so investors and tourists would feel secure and return. However, while striving to build confidence in the country's future, Lebanon must deal with ongoing Middle East violence that makes investors skeptical. Retaliation for Palestinian attacks launched from Lebanon has proven costly. Israeli bombing of power stations near Beirut in June 1999 and February 2000 resulted in $40 million in damages.

> **Until the breakup of the Ottoman Empire, the people of Lebanon used Turkish and Egyptian currency. Under the French mandate, a new Lebanese currency—the Lebanese pound—was linked to the French franc and the French economy. The Lebanese pound was interchangeable with the Syrian pound (Syria was also under French mandate) until a 1937 agreement between the Banque du Liban (Lebanon's Central Bank) and the Bank of Syria separated the two.**

The government collected donations to pay for reconstruction. Billionaire Prince Alwaleed bin Talal bin Abdul-Aziz al-Saud of Saudi Arabia paid to rebuild power stations. The Iranian government gave funds to rebuild bridges that had been destroyed. In May 2002, the World Bank lent Lebanon $45 million to repair water and power services in 30 villages near Baalbek.

Economic growth has been slow. Because of continued instability, foreign companies—both from the Arab world and the West—have been reluctant to invest in Lebanon. For example, in 1998 the Al Habtoor Group, based in the United Arab Emirates, canceled plans to invest $200 million on a hotel and resort complex in Beirut.

About 70 percent of Lebanon's employed labor force works in industry, commerce, and services; the government employs 10 percent of the people, while agriculture employs 20 percent.

The illicit narcotics trade—opium, hashish, and heroin—has become a large part of Lebanon's economy. Before the civil war, hashish cultivation was common in the Bekaa Valley. Opium and cannabis grown in the eastern Bekaa Valley from 1975 to 1990 generated about $500 million per year. Economics dominated the drug trade, but during the war some Lebanese turned to drug use and became addicts. As part of a major anti-drug campaign, authorities cracked down on farming of illegal drug crops after the war, but some farmers refused to quit—these crops were the only way they could make a living. To restrict the trade, Lebanese police have worked to arrest drug traffickers and destroy the fields of illicit crops.

Merchandise exports from Lebanon dropped from 23 percent of GDP in 1989 to 4 percent in 2000. Among measures to improve trade taken in late 2000, the government reduced customs duties.

The government also took steps to reduce its soaring debt, which rose 16.5 percent in 2001, lowering international confidence and making investors cautious. Measures included increased gasoline taxes, reduced government expenditures (particularly salaries and government subsidies), and a 10 percent value-added tax (VAT) on consumer goods (mainly major import items such as cars, gasoline, tobacco, clothing, and alcohol). The VAT and reduced customs duties on clothing, leather products, and tobacco were implemented on February 1, 2002. The World Bank and International Monetary Fund required the government to take these measures before they would invest more money in Lebanon's economy.

Today, economic reform in Lebanon focuses on three principles. First, economic revival and growth through the private sector;

The Economy of Lebanon

Gross Domestic Product (GDP*): $16.7 billion
GDP per Capita: $4,395
Inflation: 0.5%
Natural resources: limestone, water, iron ore, salt, arable land
Agriculture (12% of GDP): citrus, grapes, tomatoes, apples, sugar beets, potatoes, olives, and tobacco
Industry (21% of GDP): construction material, food processing, textiles and ready-made garments, furniture, and jewelry
Services (67% of GDP): government services (including health care and education), banking, transportation, retail
Foreign trade:
    Imports—$6.6 billion: foodstuffs, machinery and transport equipment, consumer goods, chemicals, textiles, metals, fuels, and agricultural food.
    Exports—$700 million: foodstuffs and tobacco, textiles, chemicals, precious stones, metal and metal products, electrical equipment and products, jewelry, paper and paper products.
Currency exchange rate: 1,511 Lebanese pounds = U.S. $1 (September 2002)

*GDP, or gross domestic product, is the total value of goods and services produced in a country annually. All figures 2001 unless otherwise indicated. Sources: World Bank; CIA World Factbook, 2002.

second, consolidation and improvement of public sector finances; and finally, currency, wage, and price stability.

Disruptions in mail service disrupt the economy. Post-war mail services were not reliable. In 1998, the government of Lebanon hired a Canadian company to rebuild its postal system and operate postal services. The government also plans to privatize telecommunications, electricity, the state airline, the seaport at Beirut, and water utilities. The savings in operating costs and proceeds from sales will be used to pay down the public debt. By the end of 2002,

Tourism historically has been an important part of Lebanon's economy, and in the decade after the civil war the government worked to promote Lebanon as a safe, interesting tourist destination. As a result, the number of people visiting Lebanon has risen dramatically over the past five years. Lebanon is one of the most popular tourist resorts among people from the Arab world; particularly after the September 11, 2001, attacks in the United States, many Arabs decided to vacation in Lebanon rather than travel to western destinations, where they were looked upon with suspicion.

the government was also considering administrative reform, as well as possible reform of the income tax system.

There are still many problems with Lebanon's economy. For example, by the spring of 2002 the national debt was $27 billion, and private hospitals had stopped admitting government-insured patients because the government owed them $159 million in overdue bills. However, there were positive signs as well. Economic reports showed growth in the country's industry, construction, and real estate sectors. Many new houses were being built in and around Beirut. In May 2002 Lebanon completed the sale of $1 billion in Eurobonds, which increased the central bank's gross foreign currency reserves. The Euro-Mediterranean Partnership Agreement, signed in 2002, was expected to open new markets for Lebanese products.

In addition, Lebanon's tourism industry continues to rebound. The Lebanese hope their beaches, restaurants, shops, nightlife, ancient ruins, and outdoor sports will attract vacationers from other Arab countries as well as from Europe. A new luxury hotel and resort complex overlooking the Mediterranean in downtown Beirut opened in the summer of 2002. Saudi Arabia's Prince Alwaleed expressed confidence in Lebanon's future by financing the $140 million project.

The United States ranks as Lebanon's fourth-largest source of imported goods. Since the travel ban expired in 1997, more than 160 American businesses have begun operating in Lebanon. These include Microsoft, General Electric, and FedEx.

A Lebanese man enjoys a cup of Arabic coffee, a popular drink throughout the Middle East. The people of Lebanon often follow traditional ceremonies when brewing and serving coffee to guests.

The People

Because Lebanon's civil war lasted more than 15 years, and sporadic fighting and occupation by Syrian and Israeli soldiers continued even after the war ended, Lebanese under 30 have grown up facing daily violence and uncertainty. Through the war years, most people tried to carry on with normal life as much as possible, obtaining their education or running a business.

Today, the Lebanese continue dealing with the impact of the long war on their society. Some say they feel numbness or malaise. Some young people have lost interest in politics. Current Lebanese visual and performing arts and writing reflect emotions about the war.

Lebanon's is an Arab culture. Although Western influences abound, especially in Beirut, more than 90 percent of the Lebanese (both Muslims and Christians) are Arabs. Most wealthy and middle-class Lebanese live in cities. They use high-tech gadgets: cell phones, personal computers, televisions, DVD players, and the Internet. Today as before the war, luxury cars are popular. A typical Beirut traffic jam is likely to include Mercedes, BMWs, Porsches, and Ferraris. Urban families may hire live-in domestic help to cook, clean, and care for children. The poor live in slums or rural villages.

The Lebanese are friendly people known for their lavish hospitality. They greet each other with handshakes and, for relatives or friends, embraces, kisses, and *salaams* (a ceremonial greeting). Close ties with extended family, known as the concept of *ahl kin*, form the strongest unit of Lebanese society for both Muslims and Christians. Family ties may have grown even stronger through the war. Many extended families live close together, in the same village or same apartment building. Through earlier generations, a married couple often lived in one house with their unmarried children and their married

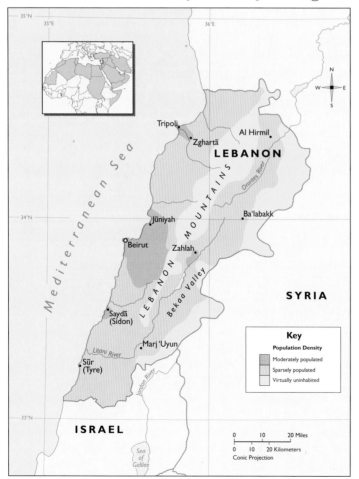

As this map shows, Lebanon's population is distributed evenly throughout the coastal region and the Bekaa Valley, with concentrations around its major cities: Beirut, Sidon, Tripoli, and Zahlah. In fact, an estimated 85 percent of Lebanese live in urban areas.

A woman works in the fields during harvest time in the agricultural Bekaa Valley. Women have more freedoms in Lebanon than in some other parts of the Arab world; however, traditions of male superiority remain.

sons and their families. Warm casual visits with extended families may include big meals and long discussions.

Families offer support and protection, as well as access to education, employment, wealth, or political power. Many former members of the national assembly inherited their seats. A business owner will hire relatives first. Those who are prosperous share with their poorer relatives. In return, family members are expected to uphold the family honor.

In Lebanese society, men and women associate freely. They attend coed schools. Women work as professionals or in unskilled jobs. Women won the right to hold public office in 1953. During the civil war, more women entered the workforce while the men were involved in the fighting. In 1997, Lebanon's national assembly ratified a convention intended to eliminate of all forms of discrimination against women. But male superiority is traditional in Arab society. When a couple marries, the man's family becomes the most important. The father, as breadwinner, heads the family, while his wife is the mother and homemaker. Male children receive preference over females.

A Shiite farmer in southern Lebanon wears traditional clothing, including the *gambaz* (tunic) and a *kaffia* (head scarf) tied with a black tasseled cord (called an *agal*).

Preserving honor in terms of how a person believes others see him or her is very important to the Lebanese. Because wealth and success are valued, status symbols such as luxury cars, swimming pools, and even the shape and size of a house, reflect their owners' economic positions.

City dwellers dress much the same as westerners. Some rural people may wear traditional clothing; for peasant women, this may be long, multicolored dresses with ankle-length trousers.

Traditional houses are made of limestone walls with an orange tile roof. During a construction boom in the early 1970s, many such houses were torn down in the frenzy to construct modern apartment buildings.

War and hard times have caused thousands of Lebanese to emigrate, many to the United States. The largest Arab community outside the Middle East is in Paris, but the second largest is in metropolitan Detroit. Most Arabs living in the Detroit area are Syrian or Lebanese; about half of them are Lebanese Christians.

FOOD

Visitors dining in a Lebanese home may feel overwhelmed by the size of the servings. The main afternoon meal can last hours. Meals begin with **mezza**, a buffet of appetizers. This can be as elaborate as 80 hot and cold hors d'oeuvres or just a salad or nuts. After the *mezza* comes a main dish of meat, chicken, or fish; a salad and rice; and dessert or fresh fruit. Raw fruits and vegetables as well as mineral water accompany most meals. The Lebanese dine late in the evening—an 11 P.M. restaurant reservation is not unusual. After the meal, diners may pass around a *nargeelies*, a pipe that filters tobacco smoke through water.

Traditional Lebanese dishes contain basic ingredients prepared again and again in different ways. Vegetables are mashed into paste and seasoned for dips. Pastries are stuffed or topped with vegetables. Vegetables are stuffed with meats. Ground meat shaped into nuggets is grilled over charcoal. Common ingredients include yogurt, cheese, cucumbers, eggplant, chickpeas, nuts, tomatoes, cracked wheat, and sesame. Parsley, mint, lemons, onions, and garlic are used to season these traditional foods. They're washed down with popular beverages—soft drinks; strong, thick Arabic coffee; locally produced wine and beer; or the national drink, a strong anise-flavored liqueur called arak.

Two types of bread are consumed in Lebanon: *khobez*, a flat round, bread found throughout the Middle East, and *marquoq*, a thin bread baked on a gas-fired domed dish. Breakfast may consist of a pizza-like baked dish of spiced cheese, squash, onions, and ground lamb on a thin crust.

Various items are served as *mezza*. One favorite is hummus, a dip of pureed chickpeas, lemon juice, garlic, and a sesame paste called tahini. A similar dip called *baba ghanoush* uses char-grilled eggplant instead of chickpeas. Falafel are deep-fried patties of spiced, ground chickpeas. *Tabouleh*, a salad, combines parsley, mint, tomato, onions, and crushed wheat dressed with lemon and olive oil. Shish kebabs are chunks of meat, green pepper, and onion grilled on a skewer. *Bahit kousa* is cracked wheat cooked with squash, peppers, and tomatoes. *Mezza* may consist of many other dishes: rice-stuffed grape leaves, cheeses, cold cuts, or lentil soup.

For main dishes, lamb is the favorite meat. *Kibbe* is nuggets of minced lamb mixed with cracked wheat and baked or fried. *Kibbe* is sometimes served raw with onion and mint. *Shawerma*, thin slices of garlic-seasoned lamb, are also popular for sandwiches. The sea supplies a variety of fish. One seafood dish, Sultan Ibrahim, consists of a small red mullet deep-fried and served with fried pita bread and sesame seed dressing. *Sayadieh* is fish cooked with rice and seasoned with onion and tahini.

One popular dessert familiar to most Americans is *baklava*, a flaky layered diamond or triangle shaped pastry filled with nuts and honey or honey-lemon syrup. Another preferred pastry is *kunafi* stuffed with sweet white cheese, nuts, and syrup.

In the cities, restaurants serve ethnic specialties from other countries, as well as fast food. Snack bars sell hamburgers, roast chicken, kebabs, *shawerma*, falafel, and soft drinks. The strong French influence has generated local patisseries, or bakeries, selling specialties such as croissants and gateaux, custard-filled cakes with candied fruits and nuts.

Shepherds watch their flock in southern Lebanon. Lamb is a popular ingredient in Lebanese cooking.

EDUCATION AND THE ARTS

Lebanon's official language is Arabic, but many Lebanese speak two or three languages. Known for casually mixing phrases from different languages, they are sometimes said to be speaking three languages at once. French was introduced during the years of the League of Nations mandate. Most government publications are published in both Arabic and French. English began gaining importance when American influence in the Middle East increased after World War II. Today it has become an essential language for business communication. In cities, signs appear mostly in English, Arabic, and French. Most middle-class Lebanese speak Arabic, French, and English; some also speak German.

The **colloquial** or everyday spoken Arabic in Lebanon varies in dialect from region to region (just as English accents vary in different areas of the United States). Classical Arabic, developed from the Qur'an, is a sacred language unifying the Arab world. It is used in formal documents, such as speeches or poetry. The Druze speak with their own unique dialect.

High literacy rates and multi-language fluency make the Lebanese culture an intellectually sophisticated one. Before the war, Lebanon's schools maintained the highest standards in the Middle East. In the 1960s Lebanon's literacy rate was 88 percent. Literacy remains strong; today, an estimated 86 percent of all those over age 15 can read and write.

Children start school in kindergarten programs at age three. They are not required by law to attend school after they are 12, but most Lebanese youngsters continue if they can. Approximately 60 percent of schools are private, and more than half of the students attend private schools. In modern computer-equipped classrooms some elementary students broaden their cultural understanding by exchanging emails with student pen pals in other countries.

The People of Lebanon

Population: 3,677,780 (July 2002 est.)
Ethnic groups: Arab 95%; Armenian 4%;
   other 1%
Age structure:
   0–14 years: 27.3%
   15–64 years: 65.9%
   65 years and over: 6.8%
Population growth rate: 1.38%
Birth rate: 19.96 births/1,000 population
Death rate: 6.35 deaths/1,000 population
Infant mortality rate: 27.35 deaths /
   1,000 live births
Life expectancy at birth:
   total population: 71.79 years
   males: 69.38 years
   females: 74.32 years
Total fertility rate: 2.02 children
   born/woman
Literacy: 86.4% (1997 est.)

All figures are 2002 estimates unless otherwise indicated.
Source: CIA World Factbook, 2002

Religion and cultural traditions are taught in churches and mosques.

Beirut has several universities and specialized colleges, including the state-owned Lebanese State University, which was founded in 1967 to teach law, medicine, the arts, and science. There are more than 100 technical and vocational schools in Lebanon. The American University of Beirut began in 1866 as Syrian Protestant College. Presbyterian missionaries built the school to provide education for people of all religions and nationalities. Its name was changed to American University of Beirut in 1920. The 70-acre campus with stone buildings and gardens overlooking the Mediterranean occupies the site of Beirut's former garbage dump. Controlled by a board of trustees in the United States, the university is known for its open intellectual atmosphere. During the wartime turmoil, staff members were often targeted for acts of violence. Another school is St. Joseph University Roman Catholic School in Beirut, which was founded in the 19th century and is run by the Jesuits, an international order of Catholic priests devoted to education.

Lebanon has produced many fine artists, writers, and performers. Generations of westerners have read *The Prophet*, a book by

Kahlil Gibran (1883–1931). The book, an English version of which was published in 1923, established Gibran as one of the most important Arabic writers of his time. The Gibran Museum (located in a converted monastery in his birthplace in the village of Bsharri, Lebanon) houses the poet's paintings, drawings, and personal belongings. Another acclaimed writer is the contemporary Lebanese playwright Georges Shehadeh, who writes in French. His works are known for their vision, humor, and the sense of brotherhood and community they deliver.

A source of great pride and enjoyment is Fairuz, the legendary Lebanese singer who rose to international stardom in the 1950s. In the course of her career, she has performed throughout the world,

Beiteddine, once an Ottoman palace, is now a hotel and museum complex.

Fairuz performs at the annual Beiteddine Festival, July 2001. The Lebanese singer has performed throughout the world and won many awards.

including concerts in other Arab countries as well as in London, Jerusalem, and at New York City's Carnegie Hall.

The Beiteddine Festival began in 1995 as a showcase for Arab performers, and then later expanded to include Western artists. The Beiteddine Palace complex with museums, gardens, and lavish early 19th-century architecture makes a dramatic setting for the festival. Located in the mountains south of Beirut, it once was the summer residence of Lebanon's president. Originally it was built for Emir Bechir Chehab II by his subjects in 1812. He lived there until his exile in 1840. Ottoman officials used the palace as a government residence. When the French took over, they housed administrative offices here. Lebanon's General Directorate of Antiquities restored the palace in 1934 and declared it an historic monument. Today, guided tours are available and part of the complex has been converted into a hotel. Other areas house museums. A ground floor museum opened in 1991. The second floor's Rashid Karami Archeological and Ethnographic Museum showcases collections of ancient pottery, Roman glass, gold jewelry, feudal period costumes, and other artifacts. Stables that once accommodated 600 horses today contain a collection of Byzantine mosaics, some dating back to the 5th and 6th centuries. Also impressive are the palace's courtyards, Turkish bath, harem suites, marble fountains, wooden balconies, mosaic floors, oriental furnishings, and carved ceilings.

Near the stables is a *khalwa*—a special room for used by the Druze for religious seclusion.

An older festival is the annual International Festival of music and drama amid the Roman ruins at Baalbek. Since it started in 1955, this festival has drawn a variety of international stars, from the legendary jazz singer Ella Fitzgerald to modern pop star Sting. Halted during the war years, the festival resumed in the mid-1990s. Another festival held before the war was an annual folk dancing festival, at which traditional Lebanese dances, such as belly dancing and a "line dance" called the *debkeh*, were performed.

Residents of Beirut have access to a variety of movies, plays, art exhibitions, and other cultural events. At its International Exhibition and Leisure Center, the city recently hosted the

Each year thousands of people visit the National Museum in Beirut, where Lebanon's cultural heritage is on display.

Sports fans in Lebanon can attend soccer matches and other events at this modern stadium, built in 1998. The stadium can hold more than 57,000 fans.

International Art Deco Fair, an exhibition of the latest home design products.

Museums in Beirut display remnants of Lebanon's vast cultural heritage. The National Museum opened in 1942 and exhibits such ancient treasures as tombs, statues, mosaics, and mummies. Although the museum was damaged during the civil war, it was renovated and reopened in 1995. The Nicolas Sursock Museum of Art houses masterpieces and antiques in an elegant mansion with stained glass windows bequeathed to the city of Beirut in 1961. Each fall this museum holds an exhibition of Lebanese painting and sculpture.

Lebanese sports fans enjoy soccer, basketball, swimming, skiing, table tennis, and volleyball. Soccer generates feverish excitement, especially at World Cup time. Fans buy flags representing their favorite team's country and hang them on balconies, in gardens, and in car windows. A Lebanese team entered the 2002 World Basketball Championship in Indianapolis. Beaches near the coastal cities make water sports popular.

Lebanon is the only Arab country to offer skiing and other winter sports. The French Army opened a ski school at Bsharri in the 1930s (the buildings now belong to the Lebanese Army). The government installed the country's first ski lift there in 1953. Today, the Cedars Ski Resort above Bsharri enjoys a long ski season (usually December through April).

The Lebanese are skilled at many old crafts. The country experienced a revival of arts and folklore in the 1960s and early 1970s. Today artisans work with brass, copper, gold, silver, leather, glass, and silk. Famed Lebanese craftwork includes jewelry, weaving, calligraphy, pottery and needlework. Artisans in the village of Jezzine specialize in carving bone-handled cutlery.

Fashion designer Elie Saab became the first Lebanese to design an Oscar winner's gown when actress Halle Berry won an Oscar in 2002. Since the 1990s, many Hollywood actresses at both the Emmy and Oscar ceremonies have worn Saab's creations. His designs mix Oriental and Western influences, incorporating rich fabrics, lace, embroidery, sequins, and silk threads. He has made wedding gowns for many prominent Arab women.

Lebanon's snow-capped mountains rise above the village of Bsharri, which is located in the northern part of the country near Tripoli. Many people of the village are Maronite Christians.

Communities

By the beginning of 2003, Lebanon's population was estimated at more than 3.7 million people (there has been no official census since 1932). The great majority of the people live in urban areas—86.6 percent, according to one Lebanese government agency. The country's largest city is its capital, Beirut, which is home to an estimated 1.6 million people. However, there are many other cities in the country with historical and cultural significance.

BEIRUT

The second half of the 20th century took Lebanon's largest city from glory to ruin; today, Beirut is rebuilding in an effort to recover those glory days. It has been inhabited for nearly 5,000 years, since the time of the Phoenicians, and claims to be the earth's oldest inhabited city.

Beirut is located on the Mediterranean Sea with mountains rising behind it; centrally located on Lebanon's coast, Beirut became the country's capital in 1920. The country's largest city with a population of 1.6 million, it also serves as chief port and trading center.

Beirut emerged as the region's most important city during the period of Roman rule. The city became known for producing fine wine and linens. Around A.D. 551, an earthquake, tidal wave, and fire destroyed much of the city, which was later rebuilt. Control over Beirut was exerted by Arabs after 635; by the Crusaders after 1110; by the Mamluks after 1291; and by the Ottomans after 1516.

During Lebanon's "Golden Age" from 1952 to 1975, Beirut served as a financial center for Arab and Western investments.

A view of downtown Beirut, Lebanon's largest city. Though the capital was devastated by the civil war, large sections of the city were rebuilt during the 1990s. Many of the buildings shown here replaced bomb-damaged office and apartment buildings.

This aerial view shows the beaches of Beirut. Since the war, a major effort has been made to clean up environmental pollution and debris from the war to once again attract vacationers and tourists to Beirut's beaches.

Beirut's sunny Mediterranean climate, striking landscape, and beaches drew tourists from the West as well as from other Arab countries. Cruise ships regularly docked at Beirut's harbor. Passengers shopped at **souks** and ate at trendy restaurants. The city's lavish resorts and exciting nightlife gave Beirut a reputation as the "Paris of the Middle East."

At the height of the tourist boom, downtown Beirut teemed with traffic congestion, elegant shops, new high-rise apartment buildings, posh Western-style hotels including the Phoenicia Hotel and Hotel St. Georges, gold shops, sidewalk cafes, nightclubs, belly dancers, terraces, sunbathers, ice cream vendors, and beach umbrellas.

The fashionable "Ras Beirut," area, a hilly peninsula near the American University of Beirut, attracted artists, poets, and writers along with businessmen and diplomats. The neighborhood featured stone houses, walled gardens, stucco apartments, balconies, patios, sidewalk cafes, and theaters. From 1950 to 1975, Beirut had more nightclubs, luxury cars, and swimming pools per square mile than any place in the world. Casino du Liban in Jounieh, Lebanon's major tourist attraction, staged million-dollar shows complete with dancers, elephants, and stallions.

Yet a short distance from the affluence and glamour, the poor lived in slums and refugee camps. Armenians, Kurds, and Palestinian refugees occupied shanties or lean-tos, without jobs or basic necessities. They suffered high unemployment and death rates. Living on the fringes of high-rolling Ras Beirut fueled anger and resentment that contributed to the eruption of the civil war.

The war began in Beirut, and the city ultimately was the scene of many battles. During the war, the **_Green Line_**, a barrier constructed of piled-up dumpsters and other refuse, split the city into a Christian eastern

These huge stone formations off the coast of western Beirut, known as Pigeon Rocks, are a famous landmark. The area, known as Raouché, is home to a variety of restaurants and shops. It is the site of the earliest known human settlement in Lebanon.

half and Muslim western half. At the war's end, the city was reduced to rubble.

Modern Beirut has begun the task of restoring its image as an international financial, commercial, and tourist center along with physical renovation and rebuilding. Construction comes largely through the efforts of billionaire Prime Minister Rafik Hariri, who hopes restoration will encourage trade and investment. Wealthy Lebanese raised millions to restore central Beirut. The old commercial downtown sector most damaged by the civil war has been razed and replaced by a new complex, Solidere, named for the company that built it. The 25-year project includes renovating old French-style buildings and restoring or reconstructing historic mosques, churches, and souks. During the rebuilding, construction workers uncovered the remains of a Roman bath, an ancient marketplace, and Roman and Byzantine houses with intact mosaics. The government spent $400 million rebuilding and expanding Beirut's international airport.

Today, restaurants, pubs, discotheques, and nightclubs playing pop music have opened along Menow Street, which runs along the former Green Line. The city bustles with banks, offices, cafes, boutiques selling designer clothes, movie theaters, and *shawerma* and falafel shops. At Christmastime the fashionable Hamra District glows with colorful lights and huge Christmas trees. Joggers and rollerbladers cruise along the seaside promenade. Vendors sell food and soft drinks. A McDonald's fast-food restaurant overlooks the Mediterranean Sea. Shops and markets sell clothing, electronic equipment, and handicrafts such as woven rugs, pottery, blown glass, caftans, and embroidered items. Beirut newspapers are published in Arabic, English, French, and Armenian. Historic landmarks include an Ottoman clock tower and Pigeon Rocks, a rock formation off the coast. Beirut also has a track for horseracing, a golf club, and a yacht club. Casino du Liban has been rebuilt and reopened in 1996. Martyr's Square in the city center marks the spot where the Turks publicly executed Lebanese citizens for anti-Turkish activities in 1916 during World War I. The Turks killed 21 Syrians and Lebanese in Damascus and Beirut. Martyr's Day is celebrated in both countries annually on May 6.

Beirut showed the world its new image in March 2002 when the city hosted an Arab League Summit for the first time in more than 35 years. In May 2002, Lebanon for the first time hosted the International Advertising Association's World Congress, a three-day trade show and conference, at the Beirut International Exhibit and Leisure Center.

TRIPOLI

Tripoli in North Lebanon is home to 350,000 people, making it the country's second-largest city. Founded by the Phoenicians in 800 B.C., it consists of Port El Mina on a peninsula with the rest of the city two miles inland. As a leading city under Roman rule, it was granted the right of self-government. The Mamluks made Tripoli a government center and founded four mosque schools there. Ruins from the Crusader and Islamic periods remain.

In modern times, Tripoli has been a focal point in the Middle East violence. In the summer of 1969, Palestinian guerrillas took over Tripoli for several days. And ordinary life stopped for Tripoli residents during a 1983 standoff between Syria and the PLO. In June of that year, Syria's president had expelled Yasir Arafat from Damascus. He and his followers were forced into Tripoli. As they set up rocket launchers and artillery, residents rushed out to find food, water, and gasoline or evacuated by highway to the south. Local leaders asked Arafat to stop the fighting but he refused. In November, Syria attempted to gain control of the PLO. About 10,000 Syrian guerrillas attacked, surrounding Arafat and his troops. Three U.S. aircraft carriers hovered off Lebanon's coast.

The center of Tripoli, Lebanon's second-largest city.

Israel and Syria mobilized reservists. Italy sent a ship to the Lebanese coast to evacuate Arafat to Tunis. Several hundred guerrillas and civilians were killed and as many more wounded.

A string of small islands is just offshore from Tripoli. The largest, called the Island of Palm Trees or Rabbits Island, contains ruins from the Roman and Crusader periods. Today the island is a nature reserve, where green turtles and rare birds are protected.

ZAHLE

A bronze statue of the Virgin Mary overlooks Zahle from a hilltop tower east of town. With a population of 150,000, Lebanon's third-largest city lies in the Bekaa Valley against a backdrop of snowcapped mountains. The Bardaouni River, a branch of the Litani, flows out of Mount Sannine into a wooded gorge. Outdoor

The name Sidon (in Arabic, Sayda) means fishing, accurately describing a historically important occupation in this picturesque port on the Mediterranean coast.

cafes with fountains and pools line the water's edge.

Founded in the early 18th century, Zahle was burned in 1777 and 1791, then pillaged and burned in 1860. After the railroad came through in 1885, the town enjoyed prosperity. The commercial capital of the Bekaa Valley, it is famed for production of fine wine. Agricultural products include grapes, fruit, and grain.

A city of old red-roofed houses, Zahle is the birthplace of some 50 writers and poets of the 20th century. The hills overlooking Zahle are the site of Bronze Age and Iron Age tombs.

SIDON

Bordered by orange, lemon, and banana plantations, Sidon (population 80,000) is Southern Lebanon's largest city.

Sidon has been the site of many important events in history. Ancient inhabitants of this important Phoenician city are believed to have also founded Tyre. After its citizens revolted in the seventh century B.C., the Assyrian king Esarhaddon razed Sidon. During a period of rule by the Persians, Sidon gained its reputation as a city of gardens. During the Roman era, Sidon was granted the right to self-government by the empire, the Apostle Paul founded a church in the area, and tidal waves and earthquakes badly damaged the city. During the Crusades, Christian knights captured Sidon only after a 47-day siege.

Above the busy market stands the 18th-century Debbane Palace, the only remaining urban Ottoman era house in Lebanon. Built by the Hammoud family in 1721, the building was split between two families who bought it in 1800. Renovation in 1920 reflected European influences. Declared an historic monument in 1968, the house was heavily damaged by armed fighters who appropriated and abused it for five years during the war. In 1999, the owners established a foundation to restore the building and establish a local museum. The palace comprises stables, gardens,

A small boat is moored in the port city of Tyre, an ancient Phoenician stronghold.

Muslims enter a mosque in Tripoli to worship. A variety of holidays, religious as well as public, are celebrated in Lebanon.

an aviary, stained-glass windows, mosaic tiles, and engraved cedar ceilings. Its most famous feature is a T-shaped reception room. An inscription within the palace reads, "Your wishes were fulfilled beyond expectation when you built this magnificent house with its incomparable setting, beautiful as a maiden resplendent on her wedding day."

TYRE

Founded sometime before 1200 B.C., Tyre was built on an island, separated from mainland by a channel. By 1100 B.C. Tyre's seamen had sailed around the Mediterranean to found colonies in Spain, Italy, and North Africa. The strongest of the Phoenician city-states, it held out long after Babylonians conquered the rest of Phoenicia in the sixth century. Tyre successfully resisted a 13-year siege by Nebuchadnezzar, the king of Babylon. Alexander the Great attacked by land and sea after spending seven months building a **causeway**. Expanded with sand, Alexander's causeway remains today. Tyre was famed for textile manufacture and production of purple dye made from the murex, a sea snail. One of the leading cities in the region during rule by the Roman Empire, it was granted self-government. Like Sidon, it was damaged during this time by tidal waves and earthquakes.

Modern Tyre sports high-rises and ancient ruins including a Crusader church, mosaic streets, and the largest Roman **hippo-drome** ever found, once the setting for chariot races. Located far to the south of Lebanon, the city of about 30,000 was the site of much fighting during the civil war.

BAALBEK

Baalbek, in the foothills of the Anti-Lebanon Mountains in the north Bekaa Valley, was founded to honor the Canaanite god, Baal. Under Roman rule, it was a winter resort called Julia Augusta Heliopolis, "City of the Sun." A Hezbollah stronghold only recently reopened to foreign visitors, Baalbek is the site of spectacular ancient ruins. These include the Acropolis, a Greek temple; an early Christian church; and temples to the Roman gods Bacchus and Jupiter (once the largest temple in the empire). To construct these temples, the Romans shipped massive granite columns from Egypt to Tripoli then transported them from the port on stone tracks. Today, the Roman cobblestone roads, city gates, and temple ruins remain.

A land mine disguised as a rock lies by the side of a road after being cleared out of a field in Beit Yahoun, May 2002. After the withdrawal of Israeli forces in the spring of 2000, a $50 million program run by the United Nations was started to clear some 400,000 land mines from southern Lebanon.

Foreign Relations

$\mathcal{T}$raditionally, Lebanon has remained friendly with its Arab neighbors and western countries, including the United States. The Lebanese government condemned the September 11, 2001, terrorist attacks and has helped the United States by arresting suspected al-Qaeda terrorists or freezing their financial assets. It has outlawed the terrorist group Asbat al-Ansar, an extremist Sunni group linked to al-Qaeda that operates out of the Ain el-Helweh refugee camp. Lebanese courts have sentenced to death *in absentia* this group's leader, Abu Muhjin. In October 2001, Lebanese police arrested two Asbat al-Ansar members allegedly plotting attacks against the U.S. and British embassies and other targets.

Still, Lebanon remains under the domination of Syria, a nation the U.S. Department of State lists as one of seven countries that support international terrorism. Lebanon's government officially opposes terrorism; however, it has permitted groups the United States considers terrorists, such as Hezbollah, the Muslim fundamentalist group **Hamas,** and Palestinian Islamic Jihad, to operate openly in Lebanon. Hezbollah receives millions of dollars each year from Iran, another country the U.S. has linked to international terrorism. Though Lebanon is among the Arab countries that have called for a U.N. conference to define and address the causes of terrorism, its government has refused the United States's request to freeze Hezbollah assets.

The United States favors Lebanese independence and promotes close ties with the country. Since 1975, America has spent $400 million on humanitarian and development programs to improve Lebanon's economic situation and security. The United States also favors withdrawal of non-Lebanese forces from the country, and the disbanding of armed militias. The United States and Israel have asked Lebanon to deploy troops to maintain order along the border.

Before Lebanon's civil war, Beirut attracted many vacationers and investors from the West. During the course of the bloody war, westerners in Beirut became frequent targets of terrorist attacks and kidnappings. By the mid-1980s, the American government considered Lebanon so dangerous it ordered Americans to leave and banned travel to the country. Some of the few who remained were taken hostage and held for years by Iranian-supported terrorists. In 1989, embassy personnel left Beirut. A new ambassador returned in November 1990. A barbed wire-barricaded embassy reopened in March 1991 with security checkpoints to limit access. Officials entered and left Lebanon via army helicopters and went out only in the company of armed guards.

Lebanese efforts to combat terrorism after the war ended prompted the U.S. state department to let the travel ban expire in July 1997. However, then-Secretary of State Madeleine Albright said that although the Lebanese had made progress in restoring order and security, Lebanon remained a dangerous place for

Americans. Though U.S. interests in Lebanon have not been attacked in recent years, random acts of political violence continue.

LEBANON AND SYRIA

Syrian troops entered Lebanon in 1975–76, during the civil war. More than 20,000 Syrian soldiers remain in the country. Because Lebanon depends on Syria's help with reconstruction, it has not been free to negotiate peace independently with Israel. The Israelis have offered to bargain with Lebanon apart from Syria, but Lebanon has refused. In December 1999 peace talks between Israel and Syria began; they ended without agreement in January 2000. Some Lebanese appreciate how the Syrian presence has restored order and safety. Others consider Syrian political control an obstacle to a free and sovereign Lebanon.

Throughout history Lebanon has often been linked politically, socially, and economically to Syria. Those ties tightened in May 1991 when the two governments signed the first treaty between their countries. The Treaty of Fraternity, Cooperation, and Coordination developed from Taif Accord references to common

Lebanese students carry anti-Syrian banners in November 2001. Syria has kept thousands of troops in Lebanon since the mid-1970s; after the withdrawal of Israeli soldiers in 2000, many Lebanese sought the removal of Syrian forces as well.

kinship, history, and interests. Later that year, Syria and Lebanon signed the Treaty of Defense and Security, an alliance against external aggression. Subsequent pacts have addressed economics, health, and education as well as politics and judicial affairs.

LEBANON, ISRAEL, AND THE PALESTINIANS

Lebanon has been severely affected by the Arab-Israeli conflict. When the State of Israel emerged from the British-run mandate for Palestine in 1948, the Arab states refused to recognize it, insisting that the Palestinian Arabs should rule the entire country. It would take 30 years before Egypt became the first Arab state to make peace with Israel (1979), followed by Jordan (in 1994).

Attempts to resolve the Israeli-Palestinian problem have failed. Under the 1992 Madrid Peace Conference, sponsored by the United States after the Gulf War, Syria and Lebanon negotiated for peace with Israel. The Oslo Accords the next year set the basis for negotiation of a final agreement on a Palestinian state in the West Bank and Gaza Strip. Neither Madrid nor Oslo, however, yielded the desired results. Since September 2000, Israel and the Palestinians have been engaged in violent conflict and negotiations are on hold.

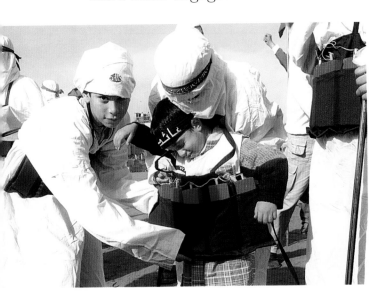

Palestinian children, dressed as suicide bombers, put fake explosives on a small child. They were taking part in a march in Ain el-Helweh, the largest Palestinian refugee camp in Lebanon. Lebanon's location bordering Israel, and its situation as the home of many Palestinians, has forced Lebanon to become involved in the violent conflict between these two parties.

The consequences for Lebanon of these long-running conflicts have been political, economic, demographic, and military. Given their own delicate religious arrangements, the Lebanese have rarely taken the lead on the Arab-Israeli issue; but they have been forced into the frontlines nonetheless.

In 1948, large numbers of Palestinians fled their homes and became refugees in Lebanon (and other neighboring countries). The U.N. Relief Agency established 17 refugee camps throughout Lebanon. The refugees lived in tents, crates, abandoned military huts, or lean-tos and ate relief rations. By the end of 1948, there were 130,000 Palestinians in Lebanon. The wealthier, educated Palestinians found a place in Lebanese society. But nearly three-quarters were poor, uneducated farmers now lacking the land they previously had worked to survive. In December 1948, U.N. General Assembly Resolution 194 called for refugees to be allowed to return home and compensated for lost property. But they could not return until peace was restored.

The Lebanese government would not allow the Palestinians to settle permanently. Since the Palestinians are Muslims, granting them citizenship would upset the distribution of power in Lebanon, which is based on religion. According to official estimates, today more than 380,000 Palestinians occupy camps in Lebanon.

Refused citizenship, the refugees maintained a "non-national" status. This meant they lacked legal rights, passports, government representation, government employment, and public education. Eventually, the Palestinians forged societies within the camps, building cinderblock houses, opening shops in their homes, peddling wares along the sidewalks, and establishing schools and clinics. Many had no jobs, no hope, and no future. They dreamed of returning to their homeland, the center of their emotions and memories. As time passed, the young Palestinians especially grew angry and turned militant. Arms were brought into the camps.

A 1964 Arab League Summit Conference in Cairo created the Palestine Liberation Organization (PLO), which employed guerrilla and terrorist tactics against Israeli military and civilians. In 1969, Yasir Arafat took over the PLO, which stepped up attacks, particularly from Jordan. By September 1970, the PLO had grown strong enough to threaten the monarchy; Jordan's King Hussein cracked down, driving Arafat and his fighters into Lebanon. In 1972, the PLO opened headquarters in Beirut. Under terms of the earlier Cairo Agreement, the PLO was supposed to allow the Lebanese government to veto attacks on Israel expected to bring retaliation; however, the PLO never honored the agreement.

Even before the PLO's move to Beirut, Lebanon had been drawn into the Israeli-Palestinian conflict. In 1968, Palestinian guerrillas based in Lebanon attacked an airliner in Athens and hijacked an Israeli plane over Italy. Israel retaliated by attacking targets within Lebanon for the first time. Although Israel directed the attacks against the Palestinians, the Lebanese lost lives and property as well. In December 1968, Israel bombed the Middle Eastern Airlines Fleet at Beirut International Airport and blew up 13 planes. Fearing further Israeli retaliation, Lebanon deployed its army to control the Palestinians. Violent demonstrations supported the Palestinians, leading to a confrontation between troops and refugees in which several people were killed. The government declared a state of emergency.

As the Palestinians increased their attacks, Israel sent bombers over South Lebanon. In May 1970, the Israelis invaded Lebanon, destroying Palestinian bases and seizing weapons and ammunition. Two weeks later, Palestinians blew up an Israeli school bus and killed 11 people. The Israelis invaded again, their forces remaining inside the border until July.

In Munich, Germany, on September 5, 1972, a group of Palestinian militants believed to have been based in Lebanon took over a dormitory and massacred 11 members of the Israeli Olympic team. A German policeman and five Palestinians died after a failed rescue attempt. Israel responded by sending commandos to Lebanon to kill the men suspected of planning the attack.

A 1973 sneak attack by Egypt and Syria on the most sacred Jewish holy day, the Day of Atonement, triggered the Yom Kippur War. Both sides suffered heavy casualties. Israel recaptured the Golan Heights and occupied some Syrian territory. The war ended with a U.N. ceasefire October 25.

In May 1974, Israeli planes attacked the Nabatieh refugee camp, killing 100 Palestinians. Israelis bombed Palestinian bases near Beirut from December 1974 through the beginning of 1975. By June, Palestinian factions were fighting each other.

Egyptian President Anwar Sadat made a huge gesture toward peace with Israel in November 1977. He flew to Israel, addressed parliament, and began peace talks with Prime Minister Menachem Begin. U.S. President Jimmy Carter arranged for U.S., Egyptian, and Israeli leaders to meet for 12 days at Camp David in September 1978. On March 26, 1979, Egypt and Israel signed a peace treaty at the White House. The treaty called for Israeli withdrawal from the Sinai Peninsula in return for peaceful relations; it also proposed Palestinian autonomy in the West Bank and Gaza. Israel returned the Sinai, but the goal of a Palestinian state stalled as the violence continued.

In 1978, in retaliation for the PLO killing of 32 Israelis, Israel invaded Southern Lebanon to drive out Palestinian terrorists. President Carter forced a withdrawal by threatening to stop aid to Israel. Approximately 2,000 Lebanese and Palestinians were killed, and 250,000 displaced. The United Nations sent in 7,000 peace-keeping troops to patrol the border.

On July 17 and 18, 1981, supporting Lebanese Phalangist militiamen, Israeli jets bombed central Lebanon, killing 200 civilians in

Beirut. President Ronald Reagan's special envoy, Philip Habib, mediated peace that lasted until June 1982 when an Israeli diplomat was shot in London by a Palestinian assailant.

A nine-week Israeli siege of southern and central Lebanon began in June 1982. Ariel Sharon, then Israel's defense minister, planned to drive the PLO out of Lebanon. He wanted a Lebanese government that would expel the PLO and make peace with Israel. The Lebanese remained divided, but some, especially in South Lebanon, were happy to be rid of the PLO. In September, Arafat and his troops were forced to evacuate under the supervision of a multinational force, including U.S. Marines. Following massacres at the Sabra and Chatilla refugee camps the force, which had been withdrawn after Arafat left, returned to keep a nonexistent peace. The United States put pressure on Israel to depart. Still the Lebanese government could not regain control of its territory unless both Israel and the Syrians left.

On August 31, 1983, the Israelis withdrew from the Shouf Mountains. Phalange forces allied with the Lebanese Army battled in Druze villages. The Maronites lost 60 villages, leaving 1,000 dead and 50,000 homeless. The United States and Syria negotiated a ceasefire on September 26, 1983. As a result, the Druze controlled the Shouf Mountains.

In September 1982, President Reagan's peace initiative called for talks on Palestinian autonomy, Palestinian self-rule in the occupied territory within five years, no new Israeli settlements, and the Israeli-occupied West Bank and Gaza Strip to be linked to Jordan. Israeli Prime Minister Begin held out for a peace treaty with Lebanon that did not involve the Palestinians. Neither man succeeded. Israel would remain in southern Lebanon for another 18 years. The United States, after a suicide bombing of its marines, left in 1984.

In November 1983, the suicide bombing of an Israeli military

Israeli Defense Force (IDF) soldiers patrol the Israel-Lebanon border near Lilach in March 2000. Israel withdrew its forces from southern Lebanon later that year.

base in Tyre killed 28 Israelis and 32 Lebanese and Palestinian prisoners. In retaliation, the Israeli Army sealed off South Lebanon by closing two bridges across the Awali River. Shiite leaders called a one-day general strike, shutting down stores and banks. Four days later the bridges reopened with vehicles stopped and inspected at checkpoints.

Except for a security zone along the border, Israel withdrew from Lebanon in 1985. Hezbollah, founded with Iranian and Syrian support, continued guerrilla attacks. Baalbek in the Bekaa Valley became a base for Islamic extremist groups. Lebanon found its territory being used by both Iran and Syria to harass Israel.

After 1996, tensions intensified. Protesting Israeli plans to expand West Bank settlements and build housing in East Jerusalem, Hezbollah continued attacking Israeli settlements. In retaliation, Israel launched Operation Grapes of Wrath. Hundreds of thousands of civilians fled South Lebanon. On April 18, Hezbollah fired mortars at an Israeli military unit near a U.N. compound at Qana. Israeli shells struck the compound and killed 102 Lebanese civilians inside. On April 27 1996, a multinational committee including representatives of Lebanon, Syria, Israel, France, and the United States negotiated a ceasefire. Both sides reached the "April Understanding," agreeing not to target civilians or attack populated areas.

Israel had long regarded its position in southern Lebanon as both protective for its Galilee region and a bargaining chip in dealing with Syria. But plagued by Hezbollah suicide bombings and booby traps, Israeli Prime Minister Ehud Barak withdrew troops from the Lebanon border security zone in May 2000. The South Lebanese Army collapsed. SLA members and their families fled the country as Hezbollah guerrillas seized control. (By the end of 2001, many of these refugees had returned to Lebanon, however.)

As Lebanon declared a national holiday, Resistance and Liberation Day, thousands of people streamed into the area. Some located graves of family members who had died during the Israeli occupation or whose bodies had been returned to their native villages by the Red Cross.

Violence soon broke out between Christian and Muslim villages, because some Christians had allied with the Israelis as protectors. Homes were razed and occupants murdered. The United Nations deployed interim forces. In August 2000, Lebanon sent in more than 1,000 police and soldiers.

Although the U.N. certified that Israel had withdrawn from all of Lebanese territory, the Lebanese government—and Hezbollah—claimed that a small area known as Shebaa Farms that contained an Israeli intelligence facility belonged to Lebanon. Hezbollah has used this claim to justify attacks on Israeli positions; Syria and Iran have also helped Hezbollah militants to assemble a large rocket force near the border. Thus, Lebanon still faces a potentially disastrous military clash over which it has little control unless the Lebanese army secures the border at the risk of confrontation with Hezbollah, a growing factor in Lebanese politics.

In March 2002, Beirut hosted a significant Arab League meeting that brought a unified stand behind the Saudi proposals for peace with Israel. It was also the scene for gestures of conciliation between Iraq and the Gulf States, particularly Kuwait. Thus, Lebanon tried to continue its historic role as a meeting ground that allowed antagonists to try diplomatic initiatives.

LEBANON AND THE UNITED STATES

The United States has had a long history of good relations with Lebanon built on the foundation of educational opportunities, especially the American University of Beirut. This was reinforced politically in the 1950s. While many Lebanese disliked U.S. support of Israel, the pro-Western, anti-communist, Christian-dominated governments of Lebanon looked to the United States to protect it against attacks by others. In 1958, when pro-Nasser factions threatened to break up Lebanon, U.S. Marines landed to prevent it.

At the request of President Camille Chamoun, President Dwight D. Eisenhower sent 14,000 Marines into Beirut. On July 17, 1958, Marines landed at Khalde (Red) Beach four miles from Beirut, near the airport, and 1,500 yards from the village of Khalde. The Marines created a spectacle for workmen building a road along the beach, soft drink vendors, and vacationers swimming and sunbathing. Some villagers rode out on horseback to have a look. The spectators waved and cheered. Local boys tried to help the Marines bring their heavy equipment ashore. During the deployment, one Marine was killed by sniper

Before the French Mandate, a majority of Lebanese, Syrians, and Palestinians chose the United States as the country they wanted to guide them toward independence. When the United States decided not to join the League of Nations, France received the mandate.

fire and two others died in swimming accidents. Overall the operation succeeded and Lebanon remained intact.

A later Marine expedition as part of the international peace-keeping force deployed during Israel's invasion in 1982 turned out tragically. Their mission was to oversee the safe departure of PLO troops and establish government authority after the Israeli siege of Beirut as part of a peace deal arranged by Philip Habib. The United States also hoped to increase the Lebanese government's authority and restore order. Secretary of Defense Caspar Weinberger opposed sending troops on a nonmilitary mission in an unstable, violent country. As a concession, the Marines were to stay no longer than 30 days.

Polls showed Americans disapproved 3 to 2. Intervening in the affairs of a foreign country brought reminders of still-recent Vietnam. With so many factions fighting in Lebanon how could the Marines restore order?

Part of an American, French, and Italian force, the 800 Marines arrived on August 25, 1982. Approximately 14,000 PLO troops evacuated peacefully by land and sea and Bashir Gemayel was elected president. The Marines went home in mid-September but two weeks later, after Bashir was assassinated, the troops returned at the request of the new president, Bashir's brother Amin. Approximately 1,600 Marines arrived in Beirut on September 29. They were not responsible for protecting any part of Beirut. Ordered to fire only in self-defense, the Marines were not even allowed to load their weapons unless they were attacked.

The Americans conducted daily reconnaissance missions over the Shouf Mountains and Syrian artillery positions. On August 29, 1983, Druze artillery killed two Marines. On September 6, rocket fire killed two more Marines. On September 25, the U.S. battleship *New Jersey* joined the naval squadron in Beirut and successfully bombarded Syrian artillery positions overlooking the city.

Terrorist attacks against American and other Western interests began with the April 18, 1983, bombing of the American Embassy on Bliss Street in Beirut. At 1:05 P.M., a van loaded with explosives sped past a Lebanese police checkpoint and up a circular driveway. The explosion rattled windows in a house seven miles away, killing 63 people, including 17 Americans. Islamic Jihad claimed responsibility. Terrorist threats and sniper fire increased. Marines were assigned to protect a new embassy being built in East Beirut. At this point, seven factions were fighting. Beirut was truly a war zone, with daily shelling, sniper fire, mortar blasts, and car bombings.

U.S. Secretary of State George Schultz brokered an Israeli-Lebanese peace accord in the spring of 1983 that included an Israeli withdrawal from the Shouf Mountains overlooking Beirut. But Lebanon could not put the agreement into effect against the wishes of Syria, whose leader, Hafez al Assad, bitterly opposed it. The diplomacy proved stillborn when a dramatic event led to a U.S. departure from Lebanon altogether.

At sunup over the Shouf Mountains on a quiet Sunday morning, October 23, 1983, a powerful explosion rocked Beirut. Marine headquarters, the Battalion Landing Team building (BLT), near the airport had earlier served as Israeli headquarters. The four-story building, nicknamed "The California Hilton," slept 400 Marines. It also had a mess hall, library, chapel, gym, and administrative offices. When a 2.5-ton white Mercedes truck had approached along the highway toward the airport, broke through a gate, veered around wall of sandbags, and plowed through a sentry box straight into the lobby, the sentry fired too late. He'd needed time to load his weapon. The driver detonated 2,000 pounds of dynamite around a cylinder of compressed gasoline, creating what the FBI described as the "largest non-nuclear blast in history." The BLT was destroyed and 241 Marines killed. Hundreds of wounded were trapped under the rubble of cement and cinderblocks. In a similar, almost simultaneous, bombing nearby 56 French paratroopers were killed. American newspapers described the incident as the worst sneak attack since Pearl Harbor. Weeks later, a *Washington Post* headline described Lebanon as one of "the world's most perilous spots."

President Reagan pledged justice, but after a brief retaliation against Syrian positions, Reagan decided to end the mission.

After mortars and grenades were fired at a Marine company northeast of the Beirut airport from a Shiite Muslim suburb in February 1984, about 200 Marines were redeployed to ships offshore. Another 1,400 remained at the airport. Pro-Iranian Lebanese aimed rocket launchers at the Marines from the hills above Beirut. The last Marines left Lebanon in May 1984.

These terrible events were followed by general attacks on U.S. and Western targets. In 1984, two gunmen ambushed and killed Malcolm Kerr, president of the American University of Beirut in his office. On September 20, 1984, the bombing of the U.S. Embassy annex in East Beirut killed nine people. From 1984 to 1989, militant groups linked to Hezbollah abducted some 70 Western hostages off the streets of Beirut. Victims included Americans, French, Italians, Germans, Swiss, Russians, Britons, and an Irishman. Islamic Jihad claimed responsibility for the Kerr assassination and the kidnappings but never came forward to make demands or negotiate. President Reagan had said the United States would never allow terrorists to drive Americans out of Lebanon. After an abduction, terrorists phoned a French News Agency in Beirut and challenged his statement. Hostages were kept in cellars and apartments in Lebanon, chained to walls and isolated, and moved to other locations frequently. Some were killed, and others died in captivity. Chief Associated Press Middle East Correspondent Terry Anderson was held for nine years. Terry Waite, an Anglican lay minister, negotiated the return of ten captives before he was kidnapped. The kidnappers' only demand was for Kuwait to release

4339

An armed terrorist appears at the front door of a hijacked TWA jetliner at Beirut's airport. The June 1985 flight had been diverted to Lebanon, where some passengers were held hostage for a week. This incident, and other hijackings by Palestinian sympathizers in the mid-1980s, led many countries to condemn terrorism and implement new security measures and methods to fight terrorist activities.

17 people convicted of murder in the bombing of the U.S. and French embassies and Kuwaiti installations. Two were Lebanese and believed to be relatives of the kidnappers.

At first, the Reagan administration refused to negotiate, but in 1986 it decided to secretly use Iranian channels in order to release the hostages. (When word of the arms-for-hostages deals with Iran became public in the United States, it rocked the Reagan administration.) By 1992, all surviving hostages had been released.

In June 1985, two men with pistols and hand grenades hijacked TWA Flight 847 from Athens to Rome. For three days, they threatened to blow up the plane, forcing the pilot to fly back and forth

Lebanese prime minister Rafik Hariri shakes hands with U.S. president George W. Bush during a meeting at the White House. Lebanon's government has had a fairly good relationship with the United States over the years. However, the people of Lebanon have at times criticized U.S. involvement in the Middle East. In the photo on the opposite page, Lebanese police use water cannons to try to disperse a group of demonstrators outside the American embassy in Beirut. They were protesting U.S. air strikes against Iraq during February 2001.

between Beirut and Algiers. The hijackers collected the passengers' passports. When they saw American Navy diver Robert Dean Stethem, 23, who was assigned to the battleship *New Jersey* that had shelled the Shouf Mountains, they beat him. On the second stop in Beirut, they dragged him to the door of the plane, shot him, and dropped him onto the runway. The hijackers demanded release of 776 Shiite detainees in Israel. Reagan said no. The hijackers threatened to fly the plane to Israel and blow it up over Tel Aviv. After 17 days, the hostages were freed in exchange for release of the prisoners. In 2001, claiming not to know the whereabouts of three Hezbollah members wanted by the FBI in connection with the Flight 847 hijacking, the Lebanese government refused to turn them over to U.S. authorities or prosecute them.

U.S.-Lebanese relations remain a mix of cooperation and conflict. In April 2002, for example, Secretary of State Colin Powell visited Lebanon as part of his effort to defuse Arab-Israeli tensions; his willingness even to go to Beirut was much appreciated. The

United States has fully supported Lebanese efforts to rebuild and generally understands the country's weaknesses, including the dominant Syrian role. There remain strong differences over Lebanon's refusal to take control of its southern borders and its partial cooperation on terrorism. The Lebanese are at the mercy of strong neighbors in conflict with each other. Lebanon hopes that the United States will take its interests into account on such dangerous issues as Palestinian refugees.

CHRONOLOGY

3000 B.C.: The Phoenician cities begin to grow; trade established with Egypt.

1800: The Phoenician city-states fall under Egyptian rule.

1100: Egypt loses its control over Phoenicia; Tyre expands and becomes the leading city state.

867: Phoenicia is conquered by the Assyrians, who will control the region until B.C. 612.

590: Nebuchadnezzar II of Babylon conquers most of Phoenicia.

539: The Persians destroy the empire of Babylon and conquer Phoenicia.

334: Alexander the Great begins conquest of the Persians, which will eventually lead to Greek rule over Lebanon.

64: The Roman general Pompey conquers Syria and Lebanon, bringing them into the Roman Empire.

A.D. 35: Early Christians go to Lebanon to preach the word of Jesus. Conversion to Christianity begins.

392: Christianity becomes the official religion of the Roman Empire.

410: St. John Maron dies in Lebanon.

632: Muhammad dies, but his religion spreads throughout the Arab world.

1095: Pope Urban proclaims the first Crusade to retake the Holy Land.

1197: A slow Muslim reconquest of the Holy Land begins, culminating in the final defeat of the Crusaders in 1291.

1516: Control of Lebanon passes to the Ottoman Turks.

1593: Fakhr al Din II begins fighting for Lebanese independence; he is eventually executed by the Ottoman Turks in 1635.

1832: Egypt annexes Lebanon; eight years later Ottoman rule is restored.

1860: Fighting between Christians and Druze results in a massacre of some 10,000 Christians in the Shouf Mountains.

1915: As World War I expands, Turkey attacks Lebanon; famine wipes out more than one-third of the country's population.

1923: Lebanon falls under French mandate.

1926: The Republic of Lebanon is declared.

1943: On November 22, Lebanon receives its independence from France.

1945: Lebanon joins the Arab League and the United Nations.

CHRONOLOGY

1946: The last French troops leave Lebanon.

1948: The state of Israel is established, and Israel's War of Independence begins; thousands of Palestinians leave their homes and move into neighboring Arab states, including Lebanon, where they live in refugee camps.

1958: Pro-Arab Druze and Sunni forces try to overthrow Lebanon's government in order to unite with Egypt and Syria. The conflict ends after the United States intervenes.

1964: The Palestine Liberation Organization (PLO) is founded.

1969: Cairo Agreement signed between the government of Lebanon and the PLO, limiting guerrilla attacks over Lebanon's borders into Israel.

1975: The Lebanese civil war begins in Beirut.

1976: With the blessing of the Arab League, the Syrian army occupies Lebanon.

1978: The Lebanese Front engages the Syrians in an effort to expel them; Israel invades southern Lebanon to combat the PLO.

1982: In June Israel invades Lebanon again; the PLO is forced to leave Lebanon; Palestinian refugees are massacred at Sabra and Chatilla; an international peacekeeping force arrives in Beirut.

1983: The U.S. embassy, and barracks for U.S. and French troops in Beirut, are bombed with high loss of life.

1984: Multinational peacekeeping forces leave Lebanon.

1985: Heavy fighting in southern Lebanon begins after withdrawal of Israeli troops. A Palestinian-Druze-Shiite coalition defeats Israeli-supported Christian Lebanese forces in the south.

1988: Christians and Muslims form separate Lebanese governments.

1989: The Taif Agreement is signed on October 22, providing a framework to end the civil war.

1990: The Lebanese civil war ends, and reconstruction of the country begins.

1991: Lebanon and Syria sign the Treaty of Brotherhood, Cooperation, and Coordination on May 22; in October, the Middle East Peace Conference begins in Madrid.

1992: On October 20, the first national assembly elections in Lebanon since 1972 are held. Though they are boycotted by a majority of the Christian population, the results are upheld.

CHRONOLOGY

1993: In July, Israeli troops confront Hezbollah in Southern Lebanon.

1996: Hezbollah wins eight seats in the national assembly; in April Israel bombs Hezbollah bases in Lebanon; Palestinian guerrillas agree not to attack civilians in northern Israel.

1999: Israeli bombs bridges and power plants in Lebanon.

2000: Israeli troops withdraw from Southern Lebanon on May 24.

2002: In March, Arab League Summit is held in Beirut; border clashes escalate in April, and U.S. Secretary of State Colin Powell visits Lebanon.

2003: Members of the Arab League meet in Bahrain.

GLOSSARY

arid—excessively dry; without enough rainfall to support agriculture.

Blue Line—a United Nations–designated temporary boundary between Lebanon and Israel.

caliph—the title given to an Islamic leader believed to be descended from Muhammad and having both worldly and spiritual authority to rule.

causeway—a raised road that crosses water or wet ground.

confessional system—a political system in which power is distributed proportionally among religious groups.

colloquial—the spoken language that is used in everyday conversation.

Crusades—military expeditions undertaken by European Christians between 1095 and 1291 to recapture the Holy Land from Muslims.

Druze—member of a secretive religion stemming from Islam that is neither Muslim nor Christian. Lebanon, with a Druze population of about 300,000, is home to nearly half of the worldwide Druze total.

Gnostic—a belief that matter is evil, and that salvation comes from knowledge of spiritual truth. (The Greek word *gnosis* means "knowledge.")

Green Line—a crude barricade that divided Beirut into the Christian East and Muslim West sections during the civil war.

gross domestic product (GDP)—the total value of goods and services produced within a country in a particular year.

Hamas—a Muslim fundamentalist group founded in the Gaza Strip in 1988, which is dedicated to the destruction of Israel. The Arabic word *hamas* means courage and bravery.

Hezbollah—an organization of militant Shiite Muslims formed to oppose the 1982 Israeli occupation of Lebanon, and now one of Lebanon's largest political parties. Hezbollah (the name means "Party of God") opposes Western influences and seeks to create a Muslim fundamentalist state modeled on Iran.

hippodrome—an oval stadium used by the Romans for horse and chariot races.

infidel—someone who does not believe in another's religion.

jihad—holy war.

GLOSSARY

Levant—territory at the eastern end of the Mediterranean Sea that includes the present-day countries of Lebanon, Israel, and Syria.

mandate—an order or commission given by the League of Nations to a member nation for the establishment of a responsible government over some conquered territory.

Maronite—member of an Eastern Christian church founded by followers of St. John Maron.

mezza—a buffet of appetizers.

militant—extremely active in the defense or support of a cause, often using violence and other methods most people find unacceptable.

Mount Lebanon—"The Mountain," the central Lebanon Mountains.

Phalangist—member of a Western-oriented, mainly Christian, right wing political party.

Palestine Liberation Organization (PLO)—an anti-Israeli militia that employed guerrilla and terrorist tactics while operating from bases in Lebanon.

Shiite—a Muslim who follows the precepts of Shi'a Islam, which emerged from a split in the religion after the death of Muhammad in the seventh century. Shiites believe Muhammad's descendants are the spiritual leaders of the faith.

Sunni—a Muslim who follows Sunni Islam, the major branch of the religion. Sunni Muslims believe that spiritual leaders should be selected based on their faith, rather than through heredity.

Souk—market.

FURTHER READING

Ajami, Fouad. *Dream Palace of the Arabs: A Generation's Odyssey*. New York: Pantheon Books, 1998.

Bushrui, Suheil, and Joe Jenkins. *Kahlil Gibran: Man and Poet*. Oxford: Oneworld Publications, 2002.

Fisk, Robert. *Pity the Nation: Lebanon at War*. 3rd ed. Oxford University Press, 2001.

Fuller, Graham E., and Rend Rahim Francke. *The Arab Shi'a: The Forgotten Muslims*. New York: St. Martin's Press, 2001.

Gavin, Angus. *Beirut Reborn: The Restoration and Development of the Central District*. New York: John Wiley & Sons, 1996.

Gendzier, Irene L. *Notes from the Minefield: United States Intervention in Lebanon and the Middle East 1945–1958*. Boulder, Colorado: Westview Press, 1998.

Haag, Michael. *Syria and Lebanon*. London: Cadogan Books, 2000.

O'Ballance, Edgar. *Civil War in Lebanon, 1975–92*. New York: Macmillan, 1999.

MacKey, Sandra. *Passion and Politics: The Turbulent World of the Arabs*. New York: Dutton, 1992.

Picco, Giandomenico. *Man Without a Gun: One Diplomat's Secret Struggle to Free the Hostages, Fight Terrorism, and End a War*. New York: Times Books/Random House, 1999.

Pillar, Paul R. *Terrorism and U.S. Foreign Policy*. Washington: Brookings Institution Press, 2001.

Rabinovich, Itamar. *Waging Peace: Israel and the Arabs at the End of the Century*. New York: Farrar, Straus & Giroux, 1999.

Saad-Ghorayeb, Amal. *Hizbullah: Politics and Religion*. London: Pluto Press, 2002.

http://www.lebanonembassy.org/
Embassy of Lebanon, Washington D.C., with official news and information, a country profile, photos, links, and a welcome from the ambassador.

http://www.middleeastwire.com:8080/home.html
Find daily updates from the Middle East, searchable for news from individual countries, including Lebanon.

http://dailystar.com.lb/
The *Daily Star Online*, a daily Lebanese newspaper written in English.

http://web.naharnet.com/
News and features from Lebanon and the Middle East in English.

http://leb.net/clc/
Home page of the Chicago Lebanese Club, a society dedicated to preserving and promoting Lebanese culture, which features its newsletter, projects, resources, and links.

http://www.lebmania.com/
Site features maps, photos, research information, and recipes.

http://www.wsu.edu:8080/~dee/ISLAM/ISLAM.HTM
Information on different aspects of Muslim religion and culture.

http://www.holidays.net/ramadan/
Information on the history and traditions of Ramadan, as well as other Muslim celebrations.

INDEX

Numbers in **bold italic** refer to captions.

123

INDEX

PICTURE CREDITS

2:      © OTTN Publishing
3:      Courtesy of the Embassy of Lebanon
12:     Roland Neveu/Liaison/Getty Images
17:     Courtney Kealy/Getty Images
18:     Courtesy of the Embassy of Lebanon
21:     © OTTN Publishing
22:     Courtesy of the Embassy of Lebanon
23:     Courtesy of the Embassy of Lebanon
26:     Courtesy of the Embassy of Lebanon
29:     Norbert Schiller/Getty Images
30:     Courtesy of the Embassy of Lebanon
32:     Courtesy of the Embassy of Lebanon
33:     Courtesy of the Embassy of Lebanon
34:     Courtesy of the Embassy of Lebanon
36:     Courtesy of the Embassy of Lebanon
39:     © OTTN Publishing
43:     Hulton/Archive/Getty Images
44:     Hulton/Archive/Getty Images
47:     Courtney Kealy/Liaison/Getty Images
48:     Corbis
50:     Courtney Kealy/Getty Images
53:     Courtesy of the Embassy of Lebanon
54:     AFP/Corbis
56:     Courtney Kealy/Getty Images
59:     Courtesy of the Embassy of Lebanon
61:     © OTTN Publishing
62:     Vanessa Vick/Liaison/Getty Images
66:     both Courtesy of the Embassy of
        Lebanon

70:     Courtesy of the Embassy of Lebanon
72:     Courtesy of the Embassy of Lebanon
74:     © OTTN Publishing
75:     Courtesy of the Embassy of Lebanon
76:     Courtesy of the Embassy of Lebanon
78:     Courtesy of the Embassy of Lebanon
81:     Courtesy of the Embassy of Lebanon
82:     AFP/Corbis
83:     Courtesy of the Embassy of Lebanon
84:     Courtesy of the Embassy of Lebanon
86:     Courtesy of the Embassy of Lebanon
88:     Courtesy of the Embassy of Lebanon
89:     Courtesy of the Embassy of Lebanon
90:     Courtesy of the Embassy of Lebanon
93:     Courtesy of the Embassy of Lebanon
94:     Courtesy of the Embassy of Lebanon
95:     Courtesy of the Embassy of Lebanon
96:     Courtesy of the Embassy of Lebanon
98:     Courtney Kealy/Getty Images
101:    AFP/Corbis
102:    Courtney Kealy/Getty Images
107:    Mark H. Milstein/Getty Images
113:    AFP/Corbis
114:    Mark Wilson/Newsmakers/Getty
        Images
115:    Courtney Kealy/Newsmakers/Getty
        Images

Cover photos: (front) all three images Courtesy of the Embassy of Lebanon; (back) Courtesy
        of the Embassy of Lebanon

CONTRIBUTORS

The **FOREIGN POLICY RESEARCH INSTITUTE (FPRI)** served as editorial consultants for the MODERN MIDDLE EAST NATIONS series. FPRI is one of the nation's oldest "think tanks." The Institute's Middle East Program focuses on Gulf security, monitors the Arab-Israeli peace process, and sponsors an annual conference for teachers on the Middle East, plus periodic briefings on key developments in the region.

Among the FPRI's trustees is a former Secretary of State and a former Secretary of the Navy (and among the FPRI's former trustees and interns, two current Undersecretaries of Defense), not to mention two university presidents emeritus, a foundation president, and several active or retired corporate CEOs.

The scholars of FPRI include a former aide to three U.S. Secretaries of State, a Pulitzer Prize–winning historian, a former president of Swarthmore College and a Bancroft Prize–winning historian, and two former staff members of the National Security Council. And the FPRI counts among its extended network of scholars— especially, its Inter-University Study Groups—representatives of diverse disciplines, including political science, history, economics, law, management, religion, sociology, and psychology.

DR. HARVEY SICHERMAN is president and director of the Foreign Policy Research Institute in Philadelphia, Pennsylvania. He has extensive experience in writing, research, and analysis of U.S. foreign and national security policy, both in government and out. He served as Special Assistant to Secretary of State Alexander M. Haig Jr. and as a member of the Policy Planning Staff of Secretary of State James A. Baker III. Dr. Sicherman was also a consultant to Secretary of the Navy John F. Lehman Jr. (1982–1987) and Secretary of State George Shultz (1988).

A graduate of the University of Scranton (B.S., History, 1966), Dr. Sicherman earned his Ph.D. at the University of Pennsylvania (Political Science, 1971), where he received a Salvatori Fellowship. He is author or editor of numerous books and articles, including *America the Vulnerable: Our Military Problems and How to Fix Them* (FPRI, 2002) and *Palestinian Autonomy, Self-Government and Peace* (Westview Press, 1993). He edits *Peacefacts*, an FPRI bulletin that monitors the Arab-Israeli peace process.

JAN MCDANIEL is a former newspaper reporter and the author of more than 20 books. She and her husband live in Chattanooga, Tennessee.